The OTHER SIDE *of the* Wall

Exercising discernment
in helping the poor

ISBN: 978-1-939084-35-4

Cover and layout design: Kristi Yoder

Illustrations by Nathan Wright

Printed in the USA

Second printing: January 2016

Published by:
TGS International
P.O. Box 355
Berlin, Ohio 44610 USA
Phone: 330-893-4828
Fax: 330-893-2305
www.tgsinternational.com

TGS001173

The OTHER SIDE of the Wall

Exercising discernment in helping the poor

Gary Miller

Dedication

To the many fellow believers around the world who toil each day in extreme material poverty. I have learned so much from your patience, persistence, and desire to follow Jesus. Your generosity, though living in circumstances I can hardly comprehend, has revealed so much of my own self-centeredness. I have seen God in your lives.

Table of Contents

Foreword

The Other Side of the Wall is a "must read" for those interested in Kingdom work and concerned about blessing others at home and abroad! I found the book a challenge and an inspiration, from beginning to end.

As we approach the task of helping the poor, it is important to do so with humility. We need the wisdom of God above and the advice of our brothers around us. The work is often not a neat, easy, or quick job; rather, it is complicated and takes lots of time—that is, if one wants to do it right.

When helping the needy, we must do it in a way that helps them preserve their dignity and self-respect. Just because we have more money doesn't mean we have all the answers. We need to hear and learn from them too. And always, we need to help without bargaining away Bible principles.

Gary shares thoughts that are challenging, even to the point of making one uncomfortable. After all, when we have read the book, we know more and become more accountable. But as long as we are interested in learning how to better bless others, we can grow and learn in the task before us.

One recurring question I had while reading *The Other Side of the Wall* was this: which side of the wall is it really better to be on? We think we know which side has more difficulties. But on which side are the dangers greater? How does God see it? As I came to the end of the book, though, I felt reassured that God placed each one of us where He wanted us. Yet, we have so much to learn from His Word on how He wants us to respond, where we are and with the resources He has blessed us, to those on the other side of the wall.

We are sensitive to the fact that aid given too freely for too long can create problems of dependency. Long-term solutions to poverty must involve teaching, training, and walking alongside the poor, which take time and energy. Boxes of food, gifts of clothing, and other aid are essential to meet immediate needs in times of war, famine, and natural disaster—and to meet needs in certain categories of the needy (e.g. the handicapped, elderly, orphans, and widows). Jesus said, "Ye have the poor always with you" (Matthew 26:11). But care must be taken to not rob recipients of their incentive to work hard, think creatively, and better their own situations in a responsible way.

In early 2007, Gary Miller first contacted us with ideas for encouraging sustainability in developing countries through microfinance. His ideas for loaning small amounts of money to enable individuals to start small businesses and become self-sufficient sounded good, but there were questions. Would loan recipients repay funds loaned to them? Would such a program have a lasting impact on the lives of recipients? Could spiritual teaching and business teaching be incorporated to make the program more effective?

In the years since, we have been encouraged by the potential the SALT (Shared Accountability, Lending, & Teaching) microfinance program has to help break the cycle of chronic poverty. By teaching financial and Biblical principles simultaneously, the program is making a lasting impact on the lives of the participants. Since its inception, there has been a 98.9% repayment rate on loans. Savings groups and an agricultural component have also been added to the SALT program.

Our ultimate goal remains the same as it was when Christian Aid Ministries began in 1981. It is to point people to our Lord Jesus Christ. He is the only door to God and heaven (John 14:6). In that process, as we attempt to meet both spiritual and physical needs, we continue to learn and grow. We want to be good stewards of all God has entrusted to us through our generous supporters, making sure the funds we invest in the lives of the needy will be for their long-term good. With this goal in mind, we present *The Other Side of the Wall,* a book that helps all of us consider the best ways to match our blessings with the needs of our world.

David N. Troyer
General Director
Christian Aid Ministries

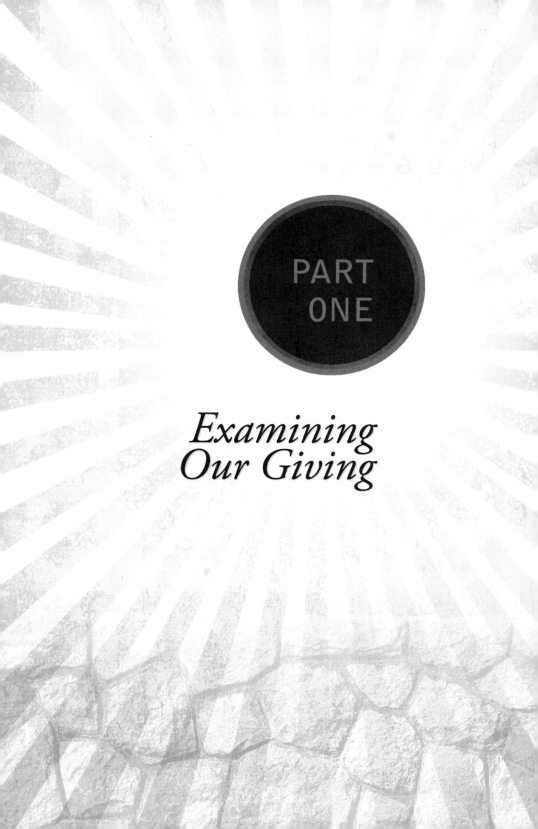

PART ONE

Examining Our Giving

The Other Side of the Wall ①

The sun slowly disappeared from view, and the scattered clouds in the west shimmered like glowing embers of a dying fire. As the inhabitants of Samaria secured their homes for the night, a sense of despair and futility settled over the city. Nobody marveled at the splendor of the sunset. Few even noticed the colors of the evening sky, for beauty often goes unnoticed when the stomach is empty.

As the twilight deepened, four men eased away from the city gate and crept along the city wall. Any onlooker would have immediately noticed the men's intense fear. They moved with cautious steps and furtive glances, always staying in the shadow of the wall.

The city of Samaria was built on a long, oval hill. As these four men warily moved farther from the city wall, they could see the hundreds of tents belonging to the invading army in the valley below them, surrounding the entire city. These men were lepers—the outcasts of Samaria. The lepers realized that death from starvation was imminent, so they decided to approach the besieging Syrian army and plead for mercy. As the men cautiously approached the outermost tents, their minds must have raced with possible entreaties. No doubt they fully expected death by the enemy, and the most they could hope for was a quick and merciful death.

Their shock was great when they discovered that the invaders had fled in haste, leaving all their belongings, food, and wealth behind. Imagine the sight! Ravenous men, destitute, starving at the bottom of the food chain in a city full of starving people, suddenly were surrounded with an abundance of food and wealth. We can only imagine how they must have attacked that food. The Bible says they satisfied their immediate hunger and then began hurriedly carrying their new-found treasure to a hiding place.

But in the middle of this running back and forth they must have stopped and looked at each other in disbelief. "Why, it was just yesterday that we were starving! Just yesterday we were longing for a crust of bread, and now we have more food than we can store. Just a short time ago we were preparing to die, and now we have more wealth than we can carry."

And then one of them saw the wall. Right there, practically beside them, was the city wall. In the middle of their festive merriment they had forgotten that, just over that wall, others were still starving. They had forgotten the dying children, the emaciated bodies, and the ravaging hunger. They had forgotten the discouragement, the misery, and the pain. They had forgotten the other side of the wall.

When they finally came to their senses, they said to each other, "Something is not right here. We are suffering from overeating, have more things than we can use, and are already struggling with storage dilemmas. And just over that wall, people are starving!"

Our world today has many similarities to this Biblical account of Samaria in the time of the prophet Elisha. In our world, a few of us have too much. We struggle with obesity, have difficulty getting closet doors shut, and have more Bibles around the house than time to read them. Meanwhile, on the other side of the wall, masses of people lack clothing, nutritious food, and a Christian witness. Some of us have many friends and find it difficult to decide which social event to attend, while others feel unwanted and live in perpetual loneliness. Some children are told to clean up their plates, while others have never seen a full one. It is a world of astonishing imbalance.

From our easy life in a developed country, we see pictures and read stories of extreme but distant poverty, and in our overwhelming abundance we occasionally look at each other and wonder: what about those on the other side of the wall? Like the lepers in the Bible, we wonder whether we are doing well. With furrowed brows we discuss the dilemma. Our world is a picture of shocking inequity. On one side of the wall, people are starving, while on the other side, people are stuffed.

Those who find themselves on the starving side of the wall have few choices. They generally lack resources, knowledge, and good role models to effect appreciable change. For them, life is extremely difficult and change seems impossible. Whether individuals are starving spiritually or physically, many have little opportunity and few options.

But what about those of us who live on the stuffed side of the wall? What about those of us who come from Christian homes, who have too much food and too many options? Where are we in this picture, and what should we be doing? What is the proper response when we discover we live on the wealthy side of the wall?

Care and Share
If you find yourself on the affluent side of the wall, you are in an extremely responsible position. Responsible like those lepers, not only because you have so much, but also because there are few with such plenty. Just picture how ridiculous it would have been for those few lepers to focus only on each other. What if days had passed while they spent their time comparing themselves with each other? What if each had compared his consumption with his neighbor's and just made sure he wasn't storing too much more than the others?

Too often this is where we find ourselves on the stuffed side of the wall. Instead of caring and sharing with those on the starving side, we use those around us as our point of reference. We find ourselves breathlessly stuffing, saving, and storing, while just over the wall, others are in great physical and spiritual need. What's more, we justify our selfish pursuits by the knowledge that those around us are involved in the same perpetual rat race.

But shouldn't a follower of the Lord Jesus be different? Shouldn't a Christian operate under a different paradigm than the self-serving world around him? The answer is obvious. True Christians will share; in fact, giving will be an evidence of following Jesus. When the Apostle Paul encouraged the wealthy church at Corinth to share, he pointed to the example of the Lord Jesus Himself. "For ye know the grace of our Lord Jesus Christ, that, though he was rich, yet for your sakes he became poor, that ye through his poverty might be rich."[a] Notice what Paul is saying. Jesus Himself was on the wealthy side of the wall at one point, yet He willingly gave up His rights, reached over the wall, and helped others.

Every person who has Christ dwelling within will share. It is the obvious result of being indwelt by the Ultimate Giver. It is the natural response of a man who understands that all he has been given is unearned and undeserved. If a believer does not have a burning desire within his heart to bless others, he has lost—or he never had—a vision of what God has done for him. Not every giver is a Christian, but every Christian is a giver.

Make Sharing a Priority

For many years the United States has been known as the country with the largest and most prosperous middle class. This is rare in a world where many countries have a vast chasm between the rich and poor. But the trends are changing in America. Statistics show that the wealthy are becoming wealthier, and the gap between the rich and poor continues to widen. Headlines warn of a shrinking middle class, and this change seems to be picking up speed.[1] Many people who were previously categorized as middle class are experiencing a reduction of money in their pockets. In July 2010, *Business Insider* published an article stating that 61 percent of Americans "always or usually" live paycheck to paycheck. This is up from 49 percent in 2008 and 43 percent in 2007.[2] Many Americans are suddenly being forced to make difficult changes, analyzing what can be eliminated from their budgets.

Many have responded to this financial change by reducing their giving. In a recent poll, 46 percent of Americans say they are giving less than they did a year ago.[3] Some families are forced to reduce their sharing simply because of previous commitments. They have mortgages, second mortgages, vehicle loans, and credit card debt. There just isn't enough

> *Not every giver is a Christian, but every Christian is a giver.*

---

[a] 2 Corinthians 8:9

extra money to share with others after all the payments.

But for others it is a matter of priorities. Many feel pressured by the affluent lifestyles of others, have become used to a high standard of living, and are reluctant to reduce that standard when their income declines. They have been sucked into this process of stuffing and storing, and they tend to forget the other side of the wall.

Surely this is a time when followers of Jesus should stand out, and sharing with others should be a priority. This is a time when we should renew our commitment to be content with food and raiment and focus all our resources on the Kingdom of God. Paul's instruction to the rich in his day was that they should be "ready to distribute."[b] I believe this means we should eagerly look for opportunities to share with those on the other side of the wall rather than deciding how little we are required to give. Caring and sharing will be a priority in the life of the individual who is following Jesus.

Begin at Home

When you think about those on the other side of the wall, where does your mind go? For many of us, our first thought is of someone on the other side of the globe. We picture people who lack food, drinking water, and the resources necessary to provide good housing and education for their children. But the starving may not be that far away; there are many who are starving right here in America.

Recently I met a man in our community who was starving. He wasn't suffering from a lack of food; rather, he was starving for friendship, affection, and family. I listened as he shared stories of people who had used and abused him in the past. He told of trusted people who had let him down, of those who were "friends" until they were getting nothing from the relationship. I was shocked to discover that he couldn't think of even one person who really cared about him.

Most of us have experienced something quite different. People have cared about us for as long as we can remember. Even though all of our life choices haven't been perfect, most people have chosen to forgive and help us along. We grew up with a network of trustworthy friends we

---

[b] 1 Timothy 6:18

could call on if we ever got in a bind. Stop for a moment and consider your situation. How many people could you call on right now if you had a need? How many would gladly listen if you wanted to talk, or send aid if you had a sudden catastrophe? If you have family and friends to whom you can appeal, you have wealth that many can only dream of having.

But sometimes "starvation" does exist within our churches. Do you have any widows in your congregation? Are there any young people who could use someone who would just spend time with them? What about local financial needs? It is possible to focus on the many needs around the globe and forget that great need may be sitting beside us on the pew.

When Jesus gave His disciples instructions on reaching out to the world with the message of salvation, He told them to start at home. Luke records Jesus saying, "Repentance and remission of sins should be preached in his name among all nations, beginning at Jerusalem."[c] Jesus didn't say they should never reach out away from home; rather, they should begin at home. Sometimes serving far away has a certain amount of glamour and excitement that may be utterly lacking in the mundane tasks near home.

Of course, we can abuse this principle. We can, like the lawyer who came to Jesus,[d] use it to define who our neighbor is. We can choose to live in a nice rural setting and resolve to help any neighbor in need, while subconsciously knowing that the odds of anyone having a serious need in our middle class locale are extremely small. A neighbor is any person whom we have the opportunity to serve,[e] and followers of Jesus will always be on the lookout for such an opportunity. But let's begin at home.

Imagining the Opportunity

I wonder how long it took for those lepers in Samaria to consider the purpose behind their discovery. I wonder how much they had eaten and how many goods they had carted off into storage before it dawned on them that living on the stuffed side of the wall carries with it a certain responsibility. This realization brought with it an initial sobriety. They knew something was wrong with their situation. They had so much, and the others had so little. But I also wonder whether they were quickly overwhelmed by a greater emotion of excitement. God had placed tremendous opportunity in the hands of these few insignificant lepers.

As they considered the plight of those who were starving on the other side of the wall, they began to realize the great potential for good that existed. They could visualize the joy of the mother who would finally have enough food for her family. They could picture the excited faces of children who could finally eat a satisfying meal.

As the possibilities dawned on them, I think they ran for the city gate to tell the others. I doubt they sat around with furrowed brows, discussing how much they were required to share. The Bible says they didn't even wait until morning. They had grasped a vision to bless those in need and could hardly wait to put that vision into action.

Conclusion

Consistently applying Jesus' teachings on our side of the wall is not easy, and we may not always know how to best respond to need. If we can grasp the magnitude both of the responsibility and the opportunity we have, I believe the Lord will open doors for us to share. None of us decided on which side of the wall to be born. We don't need to feel guilty for living here. God has placed us on this side of the wall. But He did so for a purpose, and it should be our desire to discover that purpose.

As followers of Christ, we should carry His likeness. We should bear the image of a generous, loving, and giving God. The church has not always taken that responsibility seriously. God's people have not always accomplished the goal of being the hands and feet of Jesus in His absence.

My prayer is that the Lord would give us wisdom to properly use His resources and to properly respond to need. I pray that the power of Jesus would so richly fill our lives that we, like Him, would have a desire to bless those in need. And I pray that we may learn to see our world through the compassionate eyes of our loving Heavenly Father as He daily watches over both the starving and the stuffed.

Giving— Why Do I Do It? ②

We like to give. We enjoy the feeling that follows reaching out and sharing with someone in need. The needy person may be a family member, a neighbor in distress, or someone across the ocean. Whatever the case, responding to a need is rewarding and fulfilling. We have a built-in desire to set things right. But sometimes we struggle with a secret reason for sharing. We can share to relieve our consciences.

I spend a lot of my day focusing on myself. From the time I drag myself out of bed till it's time to crawl back in, my thoughts tend to revolve around how events affect me. Opportunities, dilemmas, challenges, and problems present themselves. It is easy to drift into a mode of analyzing each choice based on how it relates to me. Choices and events swirl around like a hurricane, and I stand in the eye of the daily storm, subconsciously measuring each event by how it impacts my life.

I become dismayed at my preoccupation with self. During times of self-examination I wonder why I don't focus more on others. At those times, giving can emerge as the perfect solution—an opportunity to start focusing on things that really matter and escape this egocentric whirlpool.

Sharing with others has potential to do all of this for us. But if we are honest, we discover something else: self-focus does not automatically flee just because we give.

> *Self-focus does not automatically flee just because we give.*

I want to look at why and how we give. Ultimately, I wish to consider what God wants to see in us. Even as we examine our motives, I want to express a concern: it is possible to become so thoroughly disgusted with selfish motives that we simply stop giving. I encourage you to keep giving. Most of us have difficulty with pure motives. But if no one shared until it could be done perfectly, very little sharing would ever happen.

So go ahead and share as the Lord gives you opportunity. As you give, let the Word and Spirit of God search and purify your motives.

Examining Your Giving

When I walk out to pick up the mail, I am filled with anticipation. Potential resides in my mailbox. As I reach inside, I wonder what the little box will bring into my life. Sometimes I'll find an encouraging note from an old friend or a new picture of someone's family. Other envelopes, like the ones containing bills, aren't as exciting, but the mailbox does bring items with potential to alter my life.

The most challenging envelopes I find in the mailbox contain requests for assistance. Many good ministries use mail as a vehicle to inform donors of need, and it is important to be informed if we are to help. But some ministries go beyond merely informing, and they attempt to persuade. Heartrending articles with emotional photographs are used, and every effort is employed to convey the urgency of giving. The needs are almost endless, and we wonder just whom to help. We can't help everyone, so we sort through the various needs, throw some out, and try to help where we can.

But why do you share with some while ignoring others? What causes you to move from the "reading the interesting article" mode to actually opening your checkbook? Why do some envelopes quickly end up in the trash while others carry a message that launches a response? What actually motivates you to give?

There are several potential answers. Sometimes we respond because of prior commitment or because we feel close to the situation. Other times something inexplicable touches our hearts, and we feel God calling us to share. Perhaps we had recently been convicted to share more, and this request for help came at the right time. But beyond the issue of whom to share with, why do you share at all?

Why Do You Give?

As believers in the Lord Jesus, we give because He has done so much for us. That sounds great! But is that really why we give? As I examine my own reasons for giving, I don't always find pure motives. In fact, if I would make a list of all the times I have shared purely because of my love for God, it would be an embarrassingly short list. Even in my most noble attempt, it seems a little self-interest manages to squeeze in somewhere.

Picture motives in giving as a line going from left to the right. At the left end of the line, I see times when I give for completely self-centered reasons. I think of times when I have given only to be noticed or to receive something in return. At the right end of this line are the times when I have shared with absolutely pure motives, times when my only thought was thankfulness to God and a desire to bless others. At those times giving was a selfless act.

Me-Centered Giving

All our motives for giving could be placed somewhere along this line. In spite of our good intentions, our motives are rarely entirely pure or impure. Let us first look at times when giving is self-centered and we are hoping to receive something in return. Christian Smith, a sociology professor at Notre Dame who has conducted extensive research on the topic of philanthropy, recently said this: "People who are generous are happier, healthier, and doing better in life. There's something about learning how to get beyond one's self and helping other people that is good for the giver."[1]

Dr. Smith is saying that those who give will be happier. We understand this. Since we are aware of this fact, how can we give without thinking of the happiness we will receive? After all, happiness is surely a goal worth giving some money to receive. Jesus even acknowledged that giving with poor motives does have some reward. Speaking of those who give to be seen, He said, "They have their reward."[a] There is some limited benefit to the giver even though the motives for giving are poor.

Relief From Guilt

What about relief from guilt? You pull one of those high-pressure advertisements out of the mailbox, and right on the front, staring at you with

---

[a] Matthew 6:2

a haunted gaze, is a forlorn child. Bold print proclaims, "For only $25 you could change a life forever." You try to look away from the child's penetrating stare or quickly turn the page, hoping for a distraction. But it is hard to shake off that visual image. Finally you give the money just to relieve yourself of guilt. Twenty-five dollars can be a small price for relief. But again, was it really the child you were concerned about? Giving to relieve guilt can be another form of me-centered giving. Of course, there may be nothing wrong with giving because of guilt. But we should be honest regarding our motives.

Even with the best of intentions, we find self-centeredness in our hearts. Several years ago a brother was confessing his weakness in this area to me. He described the steps he takes to keep self out, and how often he finds self creeping back in.

"When I give to others," he told me, "I always use cash to ensure that others don't know where the money came from. I place the money in an envelope, taking care to put no return address on it. I place the envelope in the middle of the other outgoing mail—and then I find myself secretly hoping that someone finds out who sent that money!

"In my mind," he continued, "I concoct all kinds of scenarios in which someone might 'accidently' discover who sent the money and imagine the glory that might come my way."

We may be wiser than to send cash in the mail, but aren't these feelings a reality in our lives many times? It is obvious that Jesus knew our hearts. A good portion of the Sermon on the Mount teaches the importance of good motives while doing good deeds. This is a big issue for all of us.

Social Pressure

As we continue to look at our hearts, we find another motive for giving—social pressure. Sometimes we are motivated by pressure we feel from others. As I examine my life, I must admit that some of my giving has been motivated by social pressure.

Most of our church communities have occasional work days. It might be maintenance at the church house or a building project for a widow. We all enjoy these events, but they also require sacrifice. For those of us who work away from home five days a week, Saturdays become very precious. Projects begin stacking up at home, and we are not sure how we will get everything accomplished.

Then along comes one of those work days. How many times do you go simply because of what others might think if you weren't there? If no one else would ever know whether you were present, would you still attend? What percentage of your motivation is driven by love and concern for the widow, and how much is due to social pressure?

Many people are willing to give as long as something comes back. I was recently in a large hospital and noticed a display on the lobby wall telling the names of those who had donated money to build the facility. There were small brass plaques for small donations and bigger plaques for larger gifts. For extremely large endowments, huge signs announced that an entire wing had been named after the wealthy donor. These benefactors were being honored for their generosity. The hospital board had probably told them that if they donated a certain amount, they would receive a certain amount of recognition. This is obviously self-centered giving, but didn't Jesus promise a reward to those who will give to His Kingdom too?

Yes, He did, but Jesus also taught that if we choose to receive our reward now, we won't receive it later.[b] Jesus encouraged giving to demonstrate our faith. It thrills the heart of our Father when He sees His followers possess enough faith to forego present glory for future reward.

Getting Over Ourselves

We have mentioned various motivations for giving, but they all have one thing in common. Whether it is relief from the pangs of guilt, a good reputation among my peers, a future reward in heaven, or even something else, the bottom line is that I get something back.

Those of us who are parents know there are different ways a child can perform a task. Perhaps a mother tells her daughter, who happens to be reading a book, to set the table for supper. There are several ways the daughter can comply. One option is to do just the minimum because she knows things may not turn out well if she resists her mother's

---

[b] Matthew 6:1-4

command. Maybe she just lays out the plates and silverware and stops with that. There is technically nothing wrong with this; after all, the daughter did have to sacrifice her reading. When she is finished, she can reasonably argue that she complied with her mother's instruction.

Or she could go a little further in hope of reward. Maybe she dresses up the table a little, fills the water glasses, and gets some flowers from the garden, hoping Mother notices her extra effort. (We are experts at this type of service.) And if Mother doesn't immediately notice the flowers in the center of the table, the daughter might even subtly attempt to steer the conversation to nature or flowers in hope that someone might acknowledge her efforts.

Notice that in both of these acts the daughter's motive was her own good. She wasn't thinking primarily of her mother, but of what she herself might receive. Those of us who are parents also know the great blessing of seeing children go beyond what is required, serving out of appreciation for what their parents have done for them.

God-Centered Giving

I wonder whether anything thrills the heart of God more than to see His children give solely out of worship and love for Him—giving just for God! We get a glimpse of this kind of giving in the life of Zacchaeus. The Bible doesn't say that Jesus told him how much to give, or even that he needed to give anything. But Zacchaeus knew he was completely unworthy of having Jesus come to his house. Zacchaeus knew the kind of man he was and the kind of life he had lived. When Jesus reached out to him, I think he had a sudden desire to liquidate his assets for the Lord. As Zacchaeus ate his breakfast that morning, he didn't have the faintest clue what was going to happen to his finances that day. Consider his response to Jesus: "Behold, Lord, the half of my goods I give to the poor; and if I have taken anything from any man by false accusation, I restore him fourfold."[c]

In this statement I see a man whose giving had turned into an act of worship. I don't think Zacchaeus was calculating what he might get out of this in return. From a heart overflowing with gratitude, he just

---

[c] Luke 19:8

gave, expecting nothing in return.

Conclusion

Recently I was in a local park talking to an older man. He spoke of his past failures with his family, the pain of seeing his wife walk out the door years ago, and even disappointment with his church. He had attended various churches and had finally given up on church altogether. But he said something that I found sobering. He told me that all the churches he had attended seemed like they wanted something from him. They either wanted him to help swell their crowd and make them look successful, or they wanted him to help make a program work better for them, or they wanted his money to promote their agenda. But no one really seemed to care about *him*.

> *You can give without loving, but you cannot love without giving.*

Does God ever feel like that? Sometimes we give because we feel guilty, because we want to be noticed, or because we want something in return. How often do we give just for God? Moving toward God-centered giving will be a lifelong pursuit. We don't change overnight. But if we can grasp, even in a small measure, what God has done for us, giving as worship will follow. As one author said years ago, "Gratitude follows grace, like thunder follows lightning."[2]

Analyze your giving. What is your motivation? As you consider Kingdom-focused living, unclench your fist. Let your giving, whether of your time, treasure, or talents, be a response from your heart and an outpouring of your love for God. Remember, you can give without loving, but you cannot love without giving.

"God, Could We Make a Deal?" ③

He has been called the king of Hollywood philanthropy, and with connections throughout the entertainment world, Trevor Neilson is obviously a man suited for the job. With good looks, exceptional credentials, and contacts throughout the upper echelons of society and government, he has positioned himself as a philanthropic point man for the wealthy. When celebrities want to help rebuild Haiti after an earthquake, fund an orphanage in Africa, or maybe just polish their tarnished image by doing something good, Trevor is the man of choice.

With fees starting at $170,000 per year, his Global Philanthropy Group will connect you to a cause and enhance your reputation as well. As one newspaper article recently commented, Trevor "matches an A-list client to a cause, sets up a strategy and a foundation, secures meetings on Capitol Hill, brings other wealthy backers on board, and summons the media to cover every saving-the-world moment along the way."[1] He works with famous and wealthy clients like Bill Clinton, Brad Pitt, Bill Gates, and Ben Stiller. It was Trevor who fought and won the fierce bidding war for the first exclusive photos of actress Angelina Jolie's adopted son when she brought him back from Cambodia.

Almost every celebrity out there, it seems, from movie stars to sports idols, have a project or charity they promote. Using position and fame, they draw attention to the need—and in the process, draw attention to themselves. As the director for Aspen Institute, a research and advocacy organization, has said, "Almost every star has his or her cause . . . celebrities are like corporations, they make money, do good, and get their names out."[2]

All of us have read accounts of the rich and famous who donate millions of dollars to various causes. But why do they do it? Why is this segment of society, known for immorality, substance abuse, and unfaithfulness, investing time and resources in charitable causes? This group of people, perhaps more than any other, is known for its self-centeredness. Why do they even notice the poor, the orphans, and the hungry?

There is no simple answer to these questions. Some of them may be doing it, as the above researcher noted, "to get their names out." Others have undoubtedly discovered the inherent emptiness of self-focused living. Arriving at the pinnacle of their careers with more possessions, money, and fame than they know what to do with, they come to realize that the goals they have been pursuing are fickle and meaningless. These celebrities are also human, and they understand loneliness and pain. I am sure part of their giving is motivated by a desire to use their wealth and influence to help. But I suspect there is something else as well.

The Search for Relief

Earlier we addressed giving because of guilt, something all of us who live in developed countries understand. We know we have much more than most of the world has. But can you imagine the level of guilt some of these celebrities must face?

How would it affect you to know, as you fly your private jet into Rio de Janeiro for a rock concert, that tens of thousands of homeless street children are just below you, scrambling for survival and searching for breakfast in garbage cans? Imagine the disturbing thoughts that must flow through your mind as you receive millions of dollars for acting in a movie filmed in a country where people live in shacks, watch their children suffer from hunger, and have no access to clean water.

Guilt is a miserable companion. It will gnaw and churn relentlessly, and most of us will go to great lengths to find relief from guilt. I suspect many of the rich and famous find this relief by subconsciously proposing a bargain with God or their conscience, saying, in essence, "I'll give ten million dollars to this charity if you leave the rest of my life alone."

What about you? Do you ever bargain with God? Have you ever relieved your nagging conscience by offering some time, writing out a check, or donating something to a good cause? Most of us have done something of the sort. We find ways to give that assuage our conscience yet cost us very little.

The Bible tells of a time when David had sinned against the Lord, and the prophet told him to build an altar and offer a sacrifice to God. David went to Araunah, a Jebusite who owned a nearby threshing place, and asked whether he could purchase the land to offer a sacrifice to God. Araunah wished to freely give the land to David, but David wouldn't let him. "And the king said unto Araunah, Nay; but I will surely buy it of thee at a price: neither will I offer burnt offerings unto the Lord my God of that which doth cost me nothing."[a]

I have pondered David's words many times when examining my giving. I regret to admit that too often my motives in sharing are similar to the motives of the movie stars I mentioned earlier. Those people give, yet they give from their abundance, and their sharing seems to have no discernible impact on their lifestyles. I have found myself following the same pattern. In fact, I think we all can identify with this tendency. We like to give the unwanted or unneeded. We like to share spare time or extra money. We enjoy donating outdated clothes or things we no longer use. Somehow these activities relieve something within us and we feel better about ourselves and our lifestyle. It is easier to justify an affluent lifestyle when we are actively giving, even if that giving really costs us little.

But are we just bargaining with God? Have we, perhaps, forgotten that we are stewards and these possessions are not actually ours in the first place?

Hollywood Logic

Sometimes I hear discussions about another brother's choices. Perhaps someone is building an elaborate home or just purchased a vehicle that seems extravagant. Maybe he just returned from an expensive vacation, and those discussing it seem concerned. Often at the end of such a discussion, someone will say, "Well, we don't know how much he gives. Maybe he is giving a lot of money to help others, and we don't know about it."

---

[a] 2 Samuel 24:24

19

...er that if you give enough to the poor, you are entitled to use the rest at your own discretion. But isn't this Hollywood logic? Giving becomes a payment of dues. You pay a certain percentage, like under the Law, and the rest of your income is for your use.

But stewardship, in a Biblical sense, isn't simply giving to enable lavish living. Actually, stewardship

> *Biblical stewardship is simple living to enable lavish giving.*

is just the opposite. Biblical stewardship is simple living to enable lavish giving.

Stewardship involves deliberately choosing to make sacrifices in my life to facilitate my ultimate desire to be a builder in the Kingdom of God. This calls for abandonment of selfish desires, and this process doesn't go well with our flesh. We struggle with this process of sanctification in our lives. It's like trying to aim at two targets at once. We want to fund Kingdom building, but there are other things we want to do with our money as well.

These two targets may seem incompatible, but for centuries man has been trying to hit them both. Bring money in for God while making the people feel good in the process. Historically, the church has tried many schemes to achieve this goal. We typically refer to these attempts as fundraisers.

Fundraisers

We read about some of those early historic attempts at fundraising with bewilderment. Many of us grew up hearing of Johann Tetzel and his success at raising funds during the time of Martin Luther. If people would put money in the church treasury, Tetzel promised, their own sins and the sins of their relatives would be forgiven. Tetzel's claims, while preposterous, had similarities to the way many organizations and churches today raise funds for their ministries.

There are many needs within the Kingdom of God. Many of these needs require money, and as we see the desperate needs both locally and around the globe, it is tempting to focus so heavily on raising funds that we forget the Scriptural teaching regarding how those funds are to be raised.

It is obvious, however, that Jesus cared about far more than just raising funds. He taught much on this subject, not only encouraging us to give, but telling us how to do it. As you think about raising funds for projects or needs, consider these Scriptural teachings. Make sure the fundraising technique you use fits within these parameters.

- **Does it encourage anonymity?** Are funds being raised in a way that keeps the donor anonymous? This isn't always possible, but the goal of Biblical giving is to take the focus off the donor and instead put it on the Lord. Jesus was very clear that we should not give with the goal of receiving glory from men.[b] As much as possible, we are to give without others knowing it. Of course, there are times when this cannot be accomplished. When Peter healed the lame man who lay daily at the gate of the temple, it would have been difficult to remain anonymous.[c] But our goal is to keep the focus off ourselves, and certain methods of raising funds do a better job of this than others. The practice of putting a donor's name on the wall, having buildings named after a benefactor, or even purchasing items at auctions where everyone knows the identity of the buyer seems to violate this basic principle. The temptation exists to receive something from the transaction other than future praise from the Father. A true steward isn't interested in the benefit that comes from giving with one's name attached. As Jesus said regarding those who give to be seen of men, "They have their reward."[d]

- **Does it honor the wealthy?** Jesus told a dramatic story about a widow who gave only two mites, and this account provides a window into the heart of God regarding giving. The book of Mark says many wealthy men were casting money into

---

[b] Matthew 6:1-4

[c] Acts 3:1-11

[d] Matthew 6:2

21

the treasury that day. But Jesus said this one poor woman had given more than any of these wealthy men.[e] This little story flies in the face of common sense and logic. We tend to honor large donors. They are the ones who really make things happen. However, Jesus honored the giving of the poor. Does your method of fundraising honor the wealthy more than the poor? Some fundraising events provide settings where an item worth a thousand dollars is sold publicly to the highest bidder for five thousand. While this kind of giving brings in a great amount of revenue, it also has a negative effect. It separates the rich and poor, honoring the wealthy. There are only so many individuals who can afford this type of purchase, and the setting provides temptation for the wealthy to receive praise of men.

Recently I saw an advertisement from an organization that helps churches design fundraisers and bring in money. What really caught my eye, though, was the fact that they didn't even try to disguise their goal of focusing on the wealthy. "In some instances," their instructions for fundraisers said, "a high-dollar ticket price makes the event exclusive and will help attract a wealthy roster of supporters." This tendency to honor the wealthy among us is nothing new. James addressed this inclination in his epistle,[f] but we still struggle with respect of persons to this day. As we consider fundraising methods, it is important to avoid this tendency.

- **Does it provide a present-day return?** All around us we see fundraising events that demand no sacrifice. Recently a church in my area put on a carnival. There were rides for the children, games for adults, and plenty of food for everyone. By purchasing tickets for this event, you could take your children to the carnival and fund the church at the same time. Aside from the issue of carnivals and entertainment, is this

[e] Mark 12:41-44
[f] James 2:1-8

22

really the way Jesus intended for His Kingdom to be funded? Do we see the apostles going door to door selling brownies or Christmas cards? I am not saying that buying something from a neighbor child who comes to your door is wrong, but I do think we need to examine some of our fundraising methods. Is it really Biblical giving when I pay ten dollars to receive something I didn't need? Are we doing what David refused to do—give when it costs us nothing?

Conclusion

Fundraising for organizations and churches is big business. But does the end justify the means? Will God bless any tactic we use as long as the money received goes to a good cause? Is revenue all that really matters?

It seems obvious, both from the words of Jesus and the example of the early church, that God cares how funds are raised. There were needs that required funds from the earliest days of the New Testament church. One of the first things these new believers did was to bring money together and form a treasury to address this issue.[g] As the church grew, so did the needs. When the Apostle Paul wrote to the church at Corinth to make them aware of the great lack in Jerusalem, he was obviously attempting to raise funds. He shared the need and encouraged the church at Corinth to give.

We must be aware of needs today as well, and someone will need to communicate these needs to others. We should be careful, though, how this is accomplished. Alleviating the great physical and spiritual needs in the world may require funds, but it is important to use the Lord's methods. Jesus spent enough time addressing methods and motives in giving that we must conclude He ascribes importance to both.

50%

---

[g] Acts 4:33-34; 6:1-6

Living and Giving With a Goal

The issue has become a public relations nightmare. It's a huge problem for one of the world's largest companies, causing an embarrassing dilemma for its owners. How should a company respond when the media continues to interview employees and publish articles telling of inhumane working conditions in your factories? How can you continue to portray your company as a world leader in technology when all these watchdog groups keep picketing your corporate offices, with the media only too eager to report the grave situation to the world? Here's the really pressing problem: how can you maintain a good public image when your own employees are so fed up with their jobs that they are committing suicide? And not just one or two employees, but many of them! They're jumping to their deaths from the factory itself!

This is the dilemma Foxconn Technology Group faced during the last few years. Foxconn is the largest manufacturer of electronics in the world. With 1.2 million employees, Foxconn is also China's largest private employer and its biggest exporter. From their massive factories, America and the rest of the world receive containers of computers, telephones, printers, and other electronic devices. Foxconn produces the popular iPhones and iPads for Apple. They also supply electronics to many other companies such as Dell, Sony, and Motorola. In fact, it is estimated Foxconn produces 40 percent of all the consumer electronics in the world.[1]

Remaining competitive in the ever-changing world of technology has not been easy. But Foxconn has succeeded by taking advantage of inexpensive labor. In Foxconn's highest-paying factories, workers earn just $1.18 per hour, and the working conditions have been described as horrific.[2] Chinese employees are required to stand in one position for hours at a time. Talking or stretching are expressly forbidden, and clocking in five minutes late results in the loss of half a day's wages. Bathroom use is watched closely. Ten minutes is the maximum time allowed and is strictly monitored by electronic key cards.

All of this was largely ignored until the spring of 2010, when a dozen workers attempted suicide within a very short time. Word spread, and like hounds on a trail, the media began sniffing out stories from frustrated employees. As the media investigated, it was discovered these were not the first suicide attempts by Foxconn's workers. At least twenty-five employees have attempted suicide since 2007, with twenty-one of them succeeding in ending their lives. Questions and accusations flew, and large American companies scrambled for cover, trying to claim innocence. But why were these Chinese workers abruptly ending their lives? Others have worked in these sweatshop settings for years. What was causing the sudden increase in depression and suicide?

On May 18, 2010, a group of academics issued an open letter calling on Foxconn and the Chinese government to help these migrant laborers. Many of these oppressed workers had come from rural areas and had nowhere else to go for employment. Part of the statement said this: "They see no other options when they enter the city to work. The moment they see there is little possibility of building a home in the city through hard work, the very meaning of their work collapses."[3]

Meaningless Living

The workers who chose to end it all did so because their jobs and lives had lost meaning. They stood hour after hour going through the same mundane motions, and they lost hope of a better future. One of the workers interviewed stood day after day helping construct Apple's famous iPad.

Yet she had no idea what the finished product was and had never even seen a completed unit.[4] Little good will come from complaining, though. Outside the factory walls there are millions of other Chinese who would gladly take their jobs should these workers walk away. So the life of these workers turns into a meaningless swirl, and hopelessness sets in. Each day the workers wake up early, work long hours to produce products none of them can even dream of owning, and then return to small shacks with pitiful paychecks in a futile attempt to provide for their families.

It is hopeless, visionless living. The Foxconn workers are doing what needs to be done, but are getting no enjoyment or fulfillment from their labors. They just have a meaningless existence.

Meaningless Giving

Sometimes as I listen to questions about giving, I am reminded of these Chinese workers. Believers in the Lord Jesus know they are supposed to be giving and probably should be giving more. Giving, however, can also become a meaningless routine. Many of us have fallen into this rut. We wonder how much we have to give, whether a certain percentage is really required, and whether the money we are giving is really doing any good. We still go through the motions, but our giving becomes lifeless, routine, and meaningless. The joy of giving has departed. This is not what God has in mind. He does not intend our giving to become a joyless, mechanical process. God has something much greater, richer, and more fulfilling in mind.

Purposeless Frugality

There is a growing awareness among believers living in developed countries that materialism is having a negative effect on our lives, families, and churches. I have noticed one prevalent reaction to this materialistic focus: people find it easy to assume that since extravagant living is wrong, God must want us all to live in poverty. Some people believe there is some kind of inherent holiness in denying themselves personal comfort and pleasure. We tend to be influenced by our culture, but God is calling us to use His Word rather than our society as our reference for decision making.

Recently I was given a book that focuses heavily on how to live inexpensively. The book has all kinds of creative ideas for frugality, and it really is an interesting read. Obviously the author has spent a lot of time coming up with ways to live with very little. But as I read through this book, I detected no motive other than frugality. Penny-pinching seemed to be a game in which thrift became the score. Each activity's success was measured by how little money went into it.

But is this really stewardship? Is there some kind of built-in blessing in finding bargains, using coupons, or discovering new ways to live without certain luxuries? Is a person who lives frugally intrinsically holier? Will God automatically pour out blessing on anyone who does without?

God addressed a similar situation many years ago. His words are found in Isaiah 58, where He gives some powerful instructions. The topic there is fasting, but the underlying principles taught are relevant to this topic of giving, living, and doing without. This chapter provides a glimpse into the heart of God on living and giving with a goal. Let's break this chapter into three basic sections and gain some insight into what God has in mind.

Verses 1–3: "We're not getting much out of this, God." The chapter begins with God vehemently expressing His displeasure with the religious activities of the children of Israel. He begins by telling Isaiah, "Cry aloud, spare not, lift up thy voice like a trumpet, and shew my people their transgression . . ." This is strong language. Clearly, God was preparing to address a serious problem.

In the second verse He talks about their tendency to say all the right things and go through all the right motions. The Israelites were seeking God daily and even said that approaching Him was their delight. But in the third verse, the people ask God a revealing question. "Wherefore have we fasted, say they, and thou seest not?" In other words, "We are fasting, God, but we don't seem to be getting much out of it!" They were religiously doing without things, but notice their goal—it was still about them. If you have chosen to live in a small house or drive an older car, why are you doing it? What is the goal? This passage is saying it is possible to do without, yet be focused on self.

Verses 4–5: "Your method of fasting wasn't my idea." In these verses God asks some questions: "Is it such a fast that I have chosen? A day for a man to afflict his soul? Is it to bow down his head as a bulrush, and to spread sackcloth and ashes under him?" We can visualize these people appearing very pious while depriving themselves. They were humbly bowing their heads and doing without things their flesh might have enjoyed. Verse four even suggests they were debating among themselves just who was fasting correctly. But God states clearly that none of this was His idea. Does God really get any pleasure in seeing us live poorly? Does He enjoy seeing His children deprive themselves? Is He excited to find one group of people doing a better job than another at living without certain luxuries? Is this the goal? No, God has more in mind than for us to see who can do without the most things. He wants us to be motivated by something higher.

Verses 6–7: "This is my vision for my people." God does want His people to fast, live simply, and give. He desires, though, that all this is done with purpose and a goal. From these verses, let's look at several goals for our giving.

> *We may try all kinds of poverty alleviation methods, but without addressing sin, we are only applying a bandage to cover the problem.*

- **Relieve the effect of sin:** ". . . to loose the bands of wickedness . . ." The root cause of pain, burdens, and struggle is sin. The underlying goal in all our giving should be to share the Gospel of Jesus Christ, the only remedy for sin. His sacrifice for us remains the only way to loose the bands of wickedness. We may try all kinds of poverty alleviation methods, but without addressing sin, we are only applying a bandage to cover the problem. This is one of the reasons humanitarian aid has fallen into disrepute among some believers. They see individuals and organizations trying to make the world a better place without dealing with the source of the problem, and these believers overreact by deciding that physical aid is a waste of precious resources and time. You will not find this response or reaction in the life of Jesus, though. Jesus didn't shy away from helping people physically. He spent much of His time meeting their natural needs, and there is still a call for His people to help physically, even as they point others to Jesus.

- **Restore and reconcile:** ". . . to undo the heavy burdens, and to let the oppressed go free . . ." Man was made in the likeness and image of God, but through sin, man has fallen from his original state. God's desire is that man be restored and reconciled to Him, and our role as ambassadors is to labor with God in this work. Paul told the church at Corinth that just as God labors to reconcile the world, we also have been given this "ministry of reconciliation."[a] When man fell in the Garden of Eden, every part of his life was shattered. His relationship with God, his relationship with others, and even his relationship with his natural world was turned upside down. Where once he experienced peace and a right relationship, man now experienced struggle and conflict. All poverty today, whether natural or spiritual, can be traced back to a broken relationship with God.

  Our role as ambassadors for Christ is to work toward reconciliation, and this is to be the ultimate goal of our giving. Whether we are using literature to bring the lost to Jesus Christ, helping out after a disaster, or funding a program that teaches a man to provide for his family, the ultimate goal is always reconciliation. People around the globe are bound by Satan in many ways. They have wrong concepts regarding their God and an improper view of their fellow man. They have been taught false ideas about how their land should be farmed and wrong concepts regarding the animal kingdom and spirit world. Our role, whether reaching out to them in person or through funding, is reconciliation. We have been called to let the oppressed go free!

- **As you reconcile, remember:** "When thou seest the naked, that thou cover him; and that thou hide not thyself from thine own flesh." The needs around us are great and the work can

[a] 2 Corinthians 5:18

seem overwhelming. Many of us have grown up in Christian homes, and we can easily develop a "not all humans are equal" mentality. After all, surely I am not on the same level as the man in India who believes that the rat that just scurried by might be his grandmother. Or the farmers in South America who still believe that a certain goddess determines how much their fields will produce in the coming year. Of course I am superior to them! Or even the man in my town who repeatedly involves himself in poor relationships and substance abuse, yet can't understand why life is treating him so unfairly. Surely I am better than this segment of society.

But here in verse seven God says that every person on this globe is of the same flesh. None of us are superior or of a different species. The only difference is that some have had parts of their lives reconciled while others have not. In reality, none of us are fully restored. We all still carry around wrong concepts regarding God, ourselves, our abilities, and even improper ideas about our fellow man. We are at different stages in this process of restoration, but we all are a work in progress. Even though we would like to think we are in some way superior to others, God ". . . hath made of one blood all nations of men . . ."[b] There is no difference, and as we look at ways to help and reconcile our fellow man, it is essential to remember that we are working with our own flesh and blood.

When we lose sight of the goal in giving, it becomes a joyless and pointless process. If we are not careful, we begin to view money as bad and something we need to be purged of. We don't feel good if we keep money, and we feel equally miserable when we give it away. But when we get a vision to use what we have to bless and reconcile our fellow man, giving becomes stimulating and inspiring. Rather than wondering how much we have to lose through giving, we find ourselves looking for ways to economize. We do this not because there

---

[b] Acts 17:26

is some inherent virtue in frugality, but because we desire restoration and reconciliation in every human heart and life. We long to see the oppressed go free!

Equality

There is another impetus that should drive our giving, and this is the concept of equality. The Apostle Paul told the wealthy church at Corinth, "For I mean not that other men be eased, and ye burdened: but by an equality, that now at this time your abundance may be a supply for their want, that their abundance also may be a supply for your want: that there may be equality."[c]

Although God has given individuals different gifts and abilities, He always has had a desire for justice and equality. We see this desire in the Law when God gave the year of jubilee. It was a time to level things out and provide opportunity for the wealthy to share with those who had less. Today the spirit of jubilee should pervade the Kingdom of God. There are so many needs, and we have been given so much. It is a wonderful time to be alive, and if you want to share with those who have less, you are living in a world of opportunity!

Conclusion

The recent downturn in the American economy has created difficulty for many people. As a result, many churches and charities have reported a decrease in donations. However, even before this economic slump, many professing Christians were giving less. Studies have been done, research papers have been compiled on the topic, and affected churches and organizations have become alarmed. Why are many Americans losing interest in giving to churches and charities?

One of the reasons is that people have lost sight of the true goal in giving. The early church took collections to help the poor, to assist struggling churches, and to further spread the Gospel, but many modern-day churches have lost their way. Huge church buildings seem to be the order of the day, and a tremendous amount of money is spent on building, maintaining, and expanding these facilities. A study released in 2005 revealed that only two cents of every dollar given to Protestant

---

[c] 2 Corinthians 8:13, 14

churches in America was going overseas.[5] In contrast, almost seventy cents of every dollar given by the church in Korea was going to help others. We have become a self-centered nation.

Examine your goal in giving. Do you have a clear purpose? Do you have a deep desire to bless and minister reconciliation to others, even as God has blessed and reconciled you? God loves a cheerful giver. He even accepts gifts from a man who would like to give but has little to share. If you want to get a picture of how God blesses the man who labors with Him in reconciliation, read the last half of Isaiah 58.

Tired of the suicides and public relations nightmares, Foxconn installed nets around their factories to catch those jumping to their deaths. Foxconn is also using more robots in their factories. Sometimes when I consider my own failures in giving, it is easy to wonder why God didn't use robots as well.

But God desires much more than mechanical giving. He desires a relationship and wants us to work with Him. As Paul told the church at Corinth, "We are laborers together with God . . ."[d] God longs for reconciliation, and if we are working with Him, reconciliation will be our goal as well.

---

[d] 1 Corinthians 3:9

Give to Him That Asketh

Once, when I had a few hours to spend between appointments in Seattle, Washington, I walked along the wharf. I bought some lunch and found a table overlooking the water. It was a beautiful day with a light breeze and sunlight reflecting off Puget Sound. Even as I began eating my lunch, I knew the odds of eating alone were slim. The wharf area in Seattle has an abundance of beggars who work the streets, attempting to extract money from tourists. I expected a visit, and I wasn't disappointed.

Roger[a] walked up to my table and asked if I had any spare change. He was down on his luck, needed some food, and was just wondering whether I could help him out. I wasn't sure just how to help the "Rogers" along the wharf, so I told him I wasn't going to give him money, but I was willing to buy his lunch if he would sit down and chat with me first. Roger considered this proposal for a moment and scanned the horizon for easier prospects. Seeing none, he settled down across the table to talk.

I was very honest with Roger. I told him I struggle with knowing how to help people like him. I described the inner conflict I have with the teachings of Jesus telling me to share, the guilt of having more than I need, and the suspicion that most of the money given to people along the wharf doesn't end up being used as intended.

Roger seemed to appreciate my openness, and before long he began to share his story. His life was similar to accounts many of us have heard before. He frankly assessed his own life and described the events that brought him to the wharf: a dysfunctional home, a string of bad choices, and a history of substance abuse. Roger showed me where he

---

[a] Names and details of stories have been changed throughout the book to protect identity.

slept each night, a place in the shrubbery just a few feet from where we were sitting. Then he concluded, "You know, I really have it pretty good here. Within just a hundred feet I can get everything I need. There is food close by, the weather along the water is fairly mild, drugs are available if I want them, and sympathetic tourists bring cash when I need it. It really isn't that bad a life, and I don't need to go anywhere. It all comes to me."

I have thought of Roger many times since that day we had lunch together. It is easy for me to draw strong conclusions after meeting someone like Roger. Surely it's obvious that he is there because he wants to be, and if he would only make good choices, his life could be much different. People like Roger make me feel a little better—after all, it seems there's little I can do to alter his situation.

But then there are others like John.

I didn't know John very long, but our brief acquaintance gave me a new picture of the homeless. He had been down the road of drugs, alcohol, and immorality, and when I met him, he was in a local Gospel mission and sick of his old life. Unlike Roger, John urgently wanted something better, and for a short time he found that "something." John attempted to make a clean break with his life. He openly confessed the Lord Jesus, was baptized, and seemed to walk victoriously. His mental ability was not as keen as most, he had never been taught a good work ethic, and he came with a tremendous amount of baggage from past relationships. But John really tried. He had a strong desire to live a victorious Christian life, and many brothers put a lot of effort into helping him. Then one day John abruptly left, and we never heard from him again.

John was different from Roger. While Roger seemed to almost revel in his freewheeling lifestyle, John wanted change. From John I got a sense of strong bondage, of a past that kept calling him back. Following Jesus and living a new life was something he desired yet found difficult. Sometimes I wonder whether we failed John. Would more accountability have helped? Would more times of prayer and seeking God together have made a difference? But John is gone, and for all I know, John and Roger may be sitting along the same curb somewhere today.

Who Are These People?

If you live close to a large metropolis, you have probably faced the issue of dealing with beggars. You exit the freeway and there by the stop sign is a man holding a sign.

 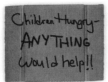  

Who are the beggars and homeless we see on the streets? Are they contented individuals like Roger? Are they people who like their present existence, enjoy an unrestricted lifestyle, and have no interest in change?

Or are most of them like John, people who desperately want something different? How are we to help them? Should we always give them something? Should we ever give them anything?

Give to Him That Asketh

Jesus said one time, "Give to him that asketh thee, and from him that would borrow of thee turn not thou away."[b] What did Jesus mean with this statement? Are we to always give something to anyone who asks? What would Jesus do?

Dealing with the homeless in America, or anywhere else, is not a simple issue. Let's begin by examining these words of Jesus. They are recorded more than once, so He must have had an important message for us to consider. Way back in the Law it was recorded, "If there be among you a poor man of one of thy brethren within any of thy gates in thy land which the Lord thy God giveth thee, thou shalt not harden thine heart,

---

[b] Matthew 5:42

nor shut thine hand from thy poor brother."[c] In the book of Proverbs we read, "Withhold not good from them to whom it is due, when it is in the power of thine hand to do it."[d] Assisting others has been God's will for us from the beginning.

The Law taught that the Israelites should help any of their brethren who were in need. But this new twist in Jesus' teaching must have been a bit of a shocker. Give to *any* man that asks? And if *anyone* wants to borrow anything I have, just let him have it? What would that look like in our lives? No wonder we feel guilty when we pass beggars. While the Law carried some disclaimers, this statement of Jesus has none. If someone asks, give to him. Period.

Give As God Gives

But in both Matthew and Luke, where this teaching is recorded, the lesson is immediately followed by another. It is a simple teaching, but it may help us understand how God wants us to give. In essence, this lesson from Jesus' teaching says this: God gives to those who are unlovely and unappreciative. He makes no distinction in His giving between good people and bad.

"He maketh his sun to rise on the evil and the good, and sendeth rain on the just and on the unjust. For if ye love them which love you, what reward have ye? Do not even the publicans the same? And if ye salute your brethren only, what do ye more than others? Do not even the publicans so?"[e]

God gives men natural blessings regardless of their response, and the message from Jesus is obvious—you go do the same thing. Go out and give as God does.

How Does God Give?

God has unlimited resources and could give us anything. Yet there are times God doesn't give what we ask for. Why does God refuse to give? If we should give like our Father, then we will need to explore how He gives and learn from Him.

---

[c] Deuteronomy 15:7

[d] Proverbs 3:27

[e] Matthew 5:45-47

Let's start with God's natural gifts. We don't find God holding back rain because of ungodliness or forbidding the sun to shine on countries that persecute Christians. He freely gives these blessings regardless of the holiness of the recipients.

Why Does God Say No?

There are spiritual blessings that God gives conditionally. He gives peace to the man who puts his trust in Him, mercy to the man who is merciful, and forgiveness to the man who forgives.

But when God tells a man no, it seems to be either because God knows it would not be a blessing to him or because giving would result in glory going somewhere else than to God.[f]

Here are a few lessons we can learn from these two teachings of Jesus.

- **Freely give.** Our Father in heaven doesn't just give rain and sunshine to those who deserve it. He doesn't restrict His giving of natural resources to the holy and upright. God shares with anyone, and so should we. I believe this is what Jesus was saying when He told us to give to him who asks. Don't discriminate. If any man is hungry or thirsty, give! Don't wait to determine whether he belongs to your fellowship or whether he is even a believer. If we see need and have no concern, we can rightly wonder whether the Spirit of God is dwelling in us.[g]

- **There is a time to say no.** Jesus qualified His statement on giving freely by teaching us to give as God does. Just as God refuses to give in certain situations, there are times we should refuse as well. If your six-year-old son asks you for a motorcycle, should you give him one? If you are mixing a pesticide in the shop and your three-year-old daughter walks in, assumes the yellow mixture is lemonade, and asks for a drink, do you give it to her? When you see someone engaging in self-destructive behavior and have reason to suspect that additional funds would encourage this, shouldn't you be careful? But before saying no, analyze your motives closely. I can think of many

---

[f] James 4:3
[g] 1 John 3:17

times, to my shame, when I refused to give to someone and my motives were not pure. I drove past someone with car trouble along the road simply because I wanted to get home quickly. I purposely avoided street people, only because I knew they would mess up my schedule.

Sometimes legitimate requests come from organizations that are doing good things, but their underlying goal is something other than honoring God. For example, they may be attempting to save forests and oceans, but they seem to worship and serve the creation more than its Creator.[h] In those cases we need to be careful as well. It is imperative, if our goal is to further the Kingdom, that we focus on giving in the name of Jesus and honoring Him in our giving.[i]

- **Time and attention may be needed more than money.**
  Francine Triplett grew up in Washington, D.C. She became involved in an abusive relationship. The day finally came when Francine decided enough was enough. Desperate, and not knowing where else to go, Francine got on a bus, rode across town, and joined the ranks of the homeless. She started out in DuPont Park where other homeless people taught her how to survive, and she quickly merged into the life of drugs and alcohol they used to help make their plight more endurable. A shelter worker and a church eventually helped her, and she was able to get a job at a local Burger King. Today she has recovered and lives a normal life.

  But as she looks back on her time living among the homeless, Francine makes an observation we should consider. One of the most difficult things she faced was being ignored. Francine tells of passing a particular woman day after day on the street and saying "Good morning," to her, but the woman never responded. "All I wanted was conversation. I didn't want food," Francine says. "I looked up at the sky and cried every night."[1]

[h] Romans 1:25
[i] Colossians 3:17

The utter loneliness of being ignored is painful for some of these people, and looking back, I know I have added to their pain. Many times I have found myself ignoring them, afraid that undue attention will bring more demands. I've been selfishly fearful that showing any interest will bring difficult questions and dilemmas, which would only conflict with my busy schedule. But surely, as followers of the Lord Jesus, we can do better! Often it is time, more than money, that is needed by the American homeless.

Recently I talked to a Christian brother who has spent much time working with America's homeless. He said many of them are swindlers and crooks, while others have legitimate needs. The brother recounted situations where people went out begging for money, trying to give a loved one a respectable funeral. Others went out begging in an attempt to provide books for their children to help them rise out of the hopelessness of their surroundings. At the end of our conversation, he said, "I wonder whether the best thing we can do is to spend more time in prayer for wisdom, and then as we confront each dilemma, try to discern the Lord's will in each situation. You won't always do it right, but there are real needs right here in America, and it is a shame for the church to just ignore them."

Conclusion

Many years ago, a brother and I tried to help a professing believer in another country who was begging for help. This person had an urgent need, and we felt pressured to provide help as soon as possible. The other brother provided the money, and it was arranged to be wired to a bank in the recipient's country.

On the very day the money was wired, we discovered that the entire request was a fraud. We were sending a rather large sum of money, and I quickly called the bank to stop the transaction. The swindler was at the counter of the bank in his country when I called, but we were able to freeze the account just in time. With the exception of the wire transfer fees, all the money was recovered and returned to the brother who had given it. That evening I called this brother to let him know what had happened. I described how close he had come to losing the money, and even though it has been many years, I can still clearly recall his comment. "My greatest fear," he said, "is that this experience will make me cynical, and next time I won't try to help."

Cynicism is a great enemy to helping those in need. I have heard discussions among well-fed people sitting around well-stocked tables, joking about some of these situations. We tend to imagine that all beggars are con artists, and we become disgusted with their poor work ethic. We suspect that anything we give will be used improperly. It is easy to assume they all have made poor choices and are just reaping what they have sowed.

But the reality is that most of us know very little about their situations. The wall is high between us, and most of us have been sheltered from the situations that have affected their course in life. We cannot even imagine how we would respond if we had been raised in their settings. Let's make sure that in all our decision making we spend time in prayer, and that the salvation of needy souls is our primary concern.

PART TWO

A Closer Look at Poverty

Defining Poverty

It was February of 2001 when I first met Robenson. Years later, the image of that crippled Haitian boy lying on the floor of his mud hut is still indelibly stamped on my mind. His legs, shriveled and useless, were tucked under his gaunt, bony body as he tried to drag himself across the filthy floor with his arms. Robenson was fifteen years old, his mother told us. He had never been to a doctor to determine his problem. Wearing a ragged, oversized purple shirt and no pants, Robenson looked up with big eyes and a pitiful smile from the dirt floor. He was the picture of poverty. He couldn't have weighed more than twenty or thirty pounds. Flies circled around him continuously. Aside from Robenson's physical handicap, he had emotional needs as well. His family and community had little regard for him. He was given food—after everyone else had eaten enough. Clothes were handed to him—after they had been worn out by others. He was obviously an unwelcome inconvenience to his family.

Robenson made a great impression on me and my children who were with me. We returned home and talked about Robenson and tried to remember him in our prayers. Several years passed before we traveled through that part of Haiti again, but when we did, we stopped at Robenson's village. We approached his hut with mixed emotions. A part of us hoped he was there and we could see him again. A greater part hoped he was gone and no longer suffering in misery. I also carried selfish concerns. I wasn't sure I could handle the sight that had so powerfully impacted me years before. But as we peered in through the doorway, there was Robenson. Still on the same dirt floor, in the same deformed position, and still surrounded by the inevitable swarm of flies. Nothing had changed! He was even wearing the same old, filthy, purple shirt.

While we may view poverty from different viewpoints and even disagree on the exact definition, I think everyone around the globe would agree: Robenson was poor. He lacked food and clothing, seemed unloved by his parents, was viewed as unproductive, and was unwanted by his community. His parents were unbelievers and showed little interest in Christianity. By almost any definition, Robenson was poor.

Defining Poverty

What is your definition of poverty? While we can all agree that Robenson was on the other side of the wall, not all situations are as straightforward. How do you determine who is poor and who isn't? Do you have a clear and concise way to make that judgment? What if Robenson would have had a clear testimony of following Jesus? Would he still have been poor? Can a man who has a vibrant relationship with Jesus really be poor?

Maybe this is the answer. Maybe we should just define poverty as relative to one's relationship with God. If this is the only criteria, though, why did the Apostle Paul speak of the "deep poverty"[a] within the churches of Macedonia? Those were vibrant churches, so why did Paul refer to them as poor?

As I listen to others using the term *poverty,* I find that it is clearly a relative description. We have people in our town who are regarded as poor. They may live in a run-down mobile home with bales of straw around the perimeter to keep the winter cold out. Or they might be on welfare and depend on a monthly check from the government. But are they really poor?

Some of these people are obese. They obviously have plenty of food, and while they may lack exercise and vegetables in their diet, they are not lacking calories. Neither are they lacking shelter from the elements. While there are nicer houses in town, I don't know of any of them being cold in the winter. Frankly, there are millions on the globe right now who would gladly swap places with these people we regard as poor. Many people in other countries long to be as wealthy as the poorest of my neighbors. So why do we refer to them as poor? From a global perspective they are rich, yet on a local level they are poor. We refer to them as poor simply because others around them have more.

---

[a] 2 Corinthians 8:2

Does Our Definition Matter?

It is tempting to wonder whether definitions really matter. From a natural point of view, there are defining walls within every society, and everyone refers to some people as rich and others as poor. In some countries those on both sides of the wall are warm and well fed, and in other countries neither side has much. So why would it matter how poverty is defined?

I propose that when trying to help the poor, your definition of poverty and what you believe causes that poverty are extremely important. How you define poverty will determine the steps you take to alleviate the problem.

A Lack of Things?

For example, if you believe that poverty is a lack of things, then the proper way to alleviate poverty is to give people the things they lack. This is simple and obvious. Once a man has what he formerly lacked, he is no longer poor, and you have fixed the problem. However, defining poverty only as a lack of things is incomplete. Some of the poorest and most miserable people I know of have lots of things.

Let's go back to the little Haitian boy, Robenson. Since he couldn't use his legs, he had to drag himself along on the ground using his elbows. As "wise" Americans, we walked into his setting that first time and immediately identified the need and formed a solution. Obviously, he needed a wheelchair. We found a wheelchair for him at a local clinic, brought it back, and presented it to his family. Robenson was one happy boy. We have pictures of him sitting in his bright red wheelchair being pushed by other children in his village. I think we all went home feeling we had helped this young man. We had provided mobility, given Robenson a sense of worth, and helped him live a more normal life. There had been a need, and we had filled it.

But did that really take care of the problem? Several years later when we returned, Robenson was back in the dirt. No wheelchair was in sight. A little investigation revealed that Robenson's father had sold it after we left. The wheelchair had funded his alcoholism.

Was giving Robenson a wheelchair the wrong thing to do? No, he did need the wheelchair. But that village, and Robenson's family, for that matter, lacked far more than just a wheelchair. Poverty is more than just a lack of things.

Consider a local example. Let's assume you have a brother in your congregation who is having trouble paying the mortgage on his house. As he stands on your doorstep asking for help, it seems clear that the thing he lacks is money since he doesn't have enough to pay his mortgage. If your underlying assumption is that poverty is a lack of things, then the obvious solution is to provide the money he lacks. But if you do this, you might come to the realization that the brother's real poverty was not merely a lack of things after all. He might be lacking management skills. Maybe he needs a better understanding of stewardship, or maybe even a less expensive home. Perhaps, more than just money, he needs someone willing to care and spend time teaching him. Maybe a spiritual mentor in his life is what he needs most, someone to meet with him occasionally and remind him of Jesus' words: "A man's life consisteth not in the abundance of the things which he possesseth."[b]

Poverty is almost always more than just a lack of things. It is important to understand this truth. But if poverty isn't just a lack of things, what is it?

Ignorance?

Some have determined that the root of poverty is ignorance. If people had more information, their problem with poverty would be solved. There are times when all of us see situations where a little more knowledge would greatly help. I remember working on a project in Haiti several years ago. Close to where we were working was a small stream, and as in most Haitian villages, the stream had multiple uses. Women came to the stream for drinking water and to do their laundry, men came for water to mix concrete, and animals came to cool off and satisfy their thirst.

I remember a woman coming to the stream and dipping her toothbrush into the murky brown water to brush her teeth. While my immune system could not have handled this, there was nothing unusual about this activity at this particular location. After all, this was the village's

---

[b] Luke 12:15

primary source of drinking water. What really shocked me was the sight of a large, partially-submerged pig just a few feet upstream from this woman. This mammoth sow was obviously enjoying a little relief from the Haitian heat, and was just as oblivious to the woman a few feet downstream as she was to the pig. The same water that washed over the filthy pig was traveling down to the woman's toothbrush.

Someone had taught this woman the importance of brushing her teeth, but she lacked some other vital information. A few scenes like this can make a person believe that ignorance is, after all, the root cause of poverty.

But if everyone had a good education, would that really take care of the world's problems? The answer to that question is very simple. While a good education is important, education alone will not fix our broken world. A report in 2012 said that 14 percent of male surgeons and 26 percent of female surgeons in America have an unhealthy dependence on alcohol.[1] Surely no one is better educated on the effects of drinking than a surgeon. Then we have the lung surgeons who smoke! They well understand the destructive power of cigarette smoking. So why do they do it? Because they still want to do it. Education is powerless to change a man's will. If you decide, however, that the root of poverty is ignorance, then your primary focus will be education.

Social Injustice?

Similar to assuming that poverty is due to ignorance, there is some truth in concluding that poverty springs from social injustice. You don't have to spend much time in underdeveloped countries to discover that much of the heartache is a result of corruption, selfishness, and greed in government. Many times mass starvation can be traced back to corrupt governments, greedy warlords, or unscrupulous businessmen exploiting the poor. The revolting practice of stealing aid intended for the needy and reselling it in the marketplace at great profit has become so common in some countries that it is expected and accepted by many. It is so common, in fact, that many government agencies refer to this practice as "traditional distribution."[2]

It is no wonder some people working in such countries conclude that social justice is the primary need. They conclude that if the people would only band together and vote their governments out of office, things would be different. Those who see social justice as the primary need tend to focus on providing legal services or other methods of empowering the poor. Services are provided for women who are oppressed by men, and aid is given to help the poor rise up and demonstrate for their rights. But is social injustice the root cause of poverty?

In America there has been a tremendous focus on social justice, yet our news media continues to inform us that the problem of poverty in America is growing worse. A recent newspaper editorial reported that "In today's America, one in fifteen people is now among the nation's poorest poor, a record high." It went on to say that "the poor in this country are more likely to stay poor" than they are in other developed countries, and "the viability of the American dream is being called into serious question."[3] For a nation that prides itself on social justice, articles like this are very revealing. Poverty is more than just a lack of social justice.

Conclusion

So what is the definition of poverty? If someone were to ask you to define what it means to be poor, what would you say? And who are the poor in our world? We want to look for the answers to these questions, but there are two things we need to remember before we move on.

First, there is some truth in many of our conclusions about poverty. A man who gains the entire world yet doesn't find Jesus is exceedingly poor.[c] On the other hand, a man who knows Jesus yet doesn't have enough food to give his children is experiencing poverty as well. In fact, one of the first issues facing the early church was dealing with the poor among them.[d] Obviously, poverty refers to more than just not knowing Jesus. It also includes a lack of basic necessities, inadequate education, and social injustice. So whatever our definition of poverty, it needs to encompass these truths.

Second, our definition of poverty is extremely important if we are

---

[c] Mark 8:36
[d] Acts 6:1

going to help others. It tends to drive our attempts at alleviating poverty. If our definition is wrong, very likely our efforts to help will fail. Although all of these views have some truth, none are complete in themselves. Giving people things does not always eliminate poverty, and in our attempt to fix poverty, we will generally create more problems. Poverty is not a simple problem; therefore, solutions may not always be obvious. So what is the definition of poverty and who are the poor in our world? Let's continue to pursue this question in the next chapter.

"It-Is-Broken" ⑦

We stood for a moment in silence viewing the twisted wreckage. A massive earthquake had devastated the little country of Haiti only a few days before, and as I looked at the incredible damage, words seemed inadequate. The epicenter of the quake had been a few miles from our microloan project, and I was out visiting clients (recipients of small loans), trying to determine where to go from here. It was hard to imagine that the pile of rubble in front of us had been a client's house just a few days before. Jagged chunks of concrete, scraps of dirty clothing, crushed inventory from their small business, and bent rebar were all that remained from his years of hard work. In contrast to this ruin, a chair salvaged from the rubble sat to one side. The chair was one small reminder of a previous, orderly life.

Samuel, a loan manager, had been taking me from house to house, and as we stopped in front of this one, I wasn't sure what to say. The damage had been so terribly complete. But as we briefly paused, Samuel turned and assessed the situation by saying in halting English, "It-is-broken."

Broken?

In spite of the surrounding devastation and heartache, I had a sudden urge to laugh. Broken? If there was ever a contest for inadequate use of verbiage, this would surely be a top contender. When we use the word *broken* in America, we use it to describe situations much less severe. But describing the horrific scene before us as *broken* seemed woefully inadequate. My family and I still chuckle at this use of the word. But really, there was nothing wrong with Samuel's choice of words. It is just that we do not normally think of brokenness as so all-encompassing. The fact is, the house really was broken. Every single wall, post, and ceiling was completely broken!

In the last chapter, we looked at two questions: what is our definition of poverty, and who are the poor in our world? As we continue to search for answers to those questions, we want to look at an event in Scripture where words also fail to convey the magnitude of the message. This event is Adam's fall into sin. The woman had eaten the forbidden fruit, and as God confronted Adam and Eve regarding their transgression, He asked them a simple question. "What is this that thou hast done?"[a] I am sure that Adam and Eve were not feeling very good at that moment. We find them backpedaling, pointing fingers, and trying to divert the blame. But I don't think they really comprehended the magnitude of what they had done. By this time they knew they had made a mistake, but what had really happened?

As a child I grew weary of hearing about Adam and Eve. It seemed all ministers felt every sermon had to start back in the Garden of Eden. But as I grow older and see more and more of this world's hurt and struggle, I realize I have underestimated the magnitude of that event. Let's look for a moment at the radical shift that took place in the Garden and the impact it had on the world.

Adam and Eve's sin had a drastic impact on relationships. They were immediately ashamed of themselves and hid from God. A little further in Genesis we read that their children were in conflict. Even the soil, something that had brought them nothing but good, began to produce thorns and thistles. Every relationship that had been good before turned sour. Their relationship with God, their relationships with each other, and even their relationship with their surrounding environment had become a mess.

Just like Samuel in Haiti, assessing the pile of rubble that had been a house, I picture God standing back and, looking at His ruined earth, sadly proclaiming, "It is broken!" What had been a wonderful and peaceful habitat for man was now a filthy, defiled, and sinful mess. It was broken!

Our world is a place of broken relationships, broken homes, and

---

[a] Genesis 3:13

broken hearts. We have grown accustomed to broken contracts, broken promises, and broken dreams. It should be obvious to anyone looking on that things are not the way they should be, or even as they once were. Adam's fall changed everything! As the Apostle Paul told the church at Rome, "For we know that the whole creation groaneth and travaileth in pain together until now.[b] In the original creation, God Himself said that everything was comprehensively good, while today it is comprehensively broken.

In his book, *Walking With the Poor,* Bryant Myers addresses the magnitude of what happened in Eden by saying this: "The scope of sin proved very broad—very holistic, if you will. It led to widespread deception, distortion, and domination in all forms of human relationships—with God, within one's self (and family), within the community and between others, and with the environment."[1]

Sin affected more than just man's relationship with God. It changed more than just his ability to take nice afternoon walks with God. Sin changed everything! It affected how Adam and Eve viewed themselves, each other, and their material world. Suddenly things didn't work the way God had originally intended.

Imagine all the firsts: the first time Adam and Eve argued, felt embarrassment and shame, or experienced the sharp pain of stepping on a thorn. Visualize the initial surprise, the puzzled looks, and the confused thoughts rushing though their minds. What was going on? Why was everything suddenly going wrong? They had abruptly entered an imperfect world.

A Dysfunctional World

In our modern society, we hear counselors refer to certain households as dysfunctional. What does that mean? It just means that a family is not functioning as it should or maybe even as it was at one time. It doesn't mean nothing good ever comes out of this home. This family may still have some good times and operate in some ways like a normal family. You may even see occasional glimpses of the healthy, vibrant family it once was. For whatever reason, the relationships are not what

---

[b] Romans 8:22

they should be, and we refer to the family as dysfunctional. As a result, everyone in that home is affected.

Our world is the same. In spite of all the problems, we still get occasional glimpses of what once was. We see the beauty of the sunrise, the engaging smile of a baby, acts of kindness between neighbors, and something within tells us this is what God intended. Like the perfectly good chair salvaged from the wreckage in Haiti, these brief glimpses remind us of a world that was. But the reality is that we live in a broken world compared to God's original design. Just as everyone in a dysfunctional home is affected, so all of us living in this world have been impacted as well. We share in the effects of this world's brokenness and poverty.

Universal Poverty

Every person, every family, every culture, and every nation carries dysfunctional traits and shares in poverty. None are excluded. But, you may say, my family or my country isn't as poor as others. I live in the United States, and we are known throughout the world as a wealthy nation. How can we be poor?

Jesus told a story one day about a man who had many possessions.[c] He began the story by describing this man's great material wealth. Everything looked good on the outside. But He finished by concluding the man was a fool and not rich at all. In fact, this man was extremely poor. Even though he had a huge crop and thought he needed to pull down his barns to build bigger ones, he had great poverty in other parts of his life. Our dysfunctional world had affected him.

For some reason, it is easy for us to understand that a man without food or clothes is poor. It is much harder for us to recognize that a man who has an abundance of material possessions, yet has no time for his wife and children, is struggling in poverty as well. Some dysfunctional traits are more noticeable, while others don't seem as bad to us. Yet the truth is that all of us have traces of poverty, regardless of our material possessions.

I first started traveling to Haiti when my older children were in their early teens. We went with work teams, and it was a good opportunity

---

[c] Luke 12:16-21

to work with the Haitian people and try to share in their lives. I must admit that on those first few trips, I viewed the Haitians as the poor and us as the wealthy. Coming from our culture, we saw them as needy and ourselves as having no lack. After a day of working on a building project, we always gathered after supper for devotions and discussion, and I began to notice something. Instead of our discussion revolving around how much these Haitians needed to learn from us, we repeatedly found ourselves discussing what we were learning from them!

> *We had come to help these desperately poor Haitians; however, their lives were exposing a different type of poverty in our own.*

We marveled at their patience, their ability to smile during disappointment, and their contentment with very little. While we became impatient if things didn't work out as planned, the Haitians seemed able to rise above little delays. While we found ourselves complaining if things weren't quite as comfortable as we were used to, our Haitian friends tolerated their discomforts without saying a word. Their prayer life also amazed us. We Americans might have spent ten or fifteen minutes in prayer, but I remember times when the Haitians were still praying long after we had finished our devotions and were in bed for the night. We had come to help these desperately poor Haitians; however, their lives were exposing a different type of poverty in our own.

It is easy for us to see poverty in other people and cultures, but the effect of poverty is universal. When man fell, more happened

> *A man with an improper regard for God has poverty in his life, regardless of the size of his bank account.*

than first meets the eye. As Bryant Myers sees it, four relationships became dysfunctional in the Garden of Eden: our relationship with our God, with our fellow man, with ourselves, and with our surrounding material world. Let's look more closely at these relationships and consider what happens when these relationships become dysfunctional.

Relationship With God

God intended our relationship with Him to be open and enjoyable. God wanted to have interaction, and I suspect He enjoyed those walks in the cool of the day even more than Adam did. Our relationship with God is of greatest importance, and each of the other three relationships must flow from this one. Get this one wrong, and every other relationship will be wrong as well. Like the rich fool, a man with an improper regard for God has poverty in his life, regardless of the size of his bank account.

Relationship With Fellow Man

Loving God and loving my neighbor cannot be separated. We are all made in the image of God, and He intends that we have proper regard for each other. The Apostle John was very clear. "If a man say, I love God, and hateth his brother, he is a liar."[d] No matter what wealth a man claims in his relationship with God, without a good relationship with his fellow man, he has poverty in his life.

Regard for Oneself

Immediately after Adam and Eve sinned in the Garden of Eden, they became self-aware and self-focused. Suddenly they were ashamed of their nakedness, became afraid, and tried to hide themselves. Since that day people have struggled with the poverty of self-centeredness and self-focus. We tend to view each day and every event from the perspective of how it will affect us. The Apostle Paul acknowledged this tendency in his letter to the Philippians and encouraged the believers to maintain a proper view of themselves. "Let this mind be in you," Paul tells them, "which was also in Christ Jesus."[e] Even Jesus was willing to humble Himself and regard Himself as a servant. In light of the example of Jesus, surely anyone who concludes he is more than a servant is thinking of himself too highly.

But we must also remember we are servants of Almighty God. What a high calling! We tend to either view ourselves as too important or totally worthless. We do have great value. It is not because of our

[d] 1 John 4:20

[e] Philippians 2:5

greatness as servants, but because of the greatness of the One whom we serve. A man who views himself as either more or less than this is experiencing poverty.

Relationship With Our Material Resources

The Apostle Paul warned the church at Corinth against misusing this world's resources when he said, "And they that use this world, as not abusing it."[f] Just as Adam was in Eden, we are to be stewards of the resources in our care. We are to use them but not abuse them. God wants us to subdue, work with, and use what He has created. But we must not destroy or abuse our environment. It still belongs to God, and He wants us to care for it properly. We see problems emerge around this globe when men ignore either of these principles. Some of God's resources are terribly abused. Men give little thought to the long-term ramifications of their abuse. The result is disease, drought, and starvation.

Others forget that material resources are only to be used. They ascribe more value to possessions than God intended. As a result, we see two types of poverty, which might at first glance appear to have no connection. Yet both stem back to an improper relationship with material resources. Let's look at these two basic instructions God gave, and what happens when either is disregarded.

- **Creation is not to be abused.** God built some basic laws of proper stewardship into creation. Material prosperity is a result of those laws being followed. But in many countries they are being trampled on, and little thought is given to stewardship of resources. Take a walk sometime on a Haitian hillside where farmers are trying to eke a living out of the rocky soil. All vegetation has been removed, the land has been given no rest, and the resulting erosion washes an estimated 10,000-15,000 hectares[2] of topsoil down the steep hillsides and out to the ocean each year. With hardly enough soil to grow crops, families struggle to survive. Many unhealthy practices like these are devastating the environment in these countries and contributing to persistent material poverty.

---

[f] 1 Corinthians 7:31

- **Creation is only to be used.** While the underdeveloped world struggles with abusing their material resources, the developed world has difficulty being content as only stewards. We tend to think of ourselves as owners and ascribe more value to material things than that which comes from their use. Secular economists use terms like *materialism* and *consumerism* to describe the greed and lack of contentment that grips men in these developed nations. This insatiable pursuit of bigger, better, and nicer things pervades our culture, and the resulting poverty is even alarming secular observers. In the book *Affluenza,* the author describes it as a disease: "A painful, contagious, socially transmitted condition of overload, debt, anxiety, and waste resulting from the dogged pursuit of more."[3]

This meaningless style of living is a different form of poverty, but individuals under its influence are still feeling its powerful effect on their lives. As an American trend forecaster and business consultant notes, "We hear the same refrain all the time from people: I have no life. I get up in the morning, daycare, eldercare, a forty-minute commute to work. I have to work late. I get home at night, there's laundry, bills to pay, and I just jam something into the microwave oven. I'm exhausted, I go to sleep, I wake up and the routine begins all over again. This is what life has become in America."[4] Another writer notes, "We are a nation that shouts at a microwave oven to hurry up."[5]

This problem may seem totally different from the man who lacks a good roof. Yet from God's perspective this kind of poverty is just as deadly and insidious. Jesus described this type of lifestyle when He said, "And the cares of this world, and the deceitfulness of riches, and the lusts of other things entering in, choke the word, and it becomes unfruitful."[g]

People experiencing this kind of poverty understand how to make the material world work for them. They are cognizant

---

[g] Mark 4:19

of the natural systems that produce material wealth. But they tend to experience deficiency in their relationships with God, their families, and themselves.

The Fifth Relationship

We have looked at four relationships that were broken when man fell, and man is directly connected in each. But there is another relationship that also needs to be noted. It is the relationship between God and His creation. When Adam sinned, God cursed the ground, causing thorns and thistles to come forth.[h] In this sphere, too, everything changed. The relationship between the Creator and His creation had been broken. And while this was a change in relationship between God and His natural creation, there were dramatic implications for man. Today we experience earthquakes, tsunamis, and all manner of other deadly natural disasters. We feel the effects of this broken relationship on a daily basis

> *The ongoing nature of sanctification shines a spotlight on the fact that all of us still have traces of poverty needing to be dealt with.*

Conclusion

Regardless on which side of the wall we find ourselves, the reality is that all of us have deficiencies in our lives. In our minds, a man who does not have a waterproof roof over his head is poor. But we find it more difficult to identify the poverty that continually drives us to obtain more and more material things or that shouts at microwaves to hurry up. For some reason we still call a man rich even though he sacrifices his family, his relationship with his fellow man, and his relationship with his God to obtain material wealth.

Even those of us who are believers feel the effects of our broken world. We come to Christ with very little knowledge of how poor we really are. God continually reveals more of our inner poverty and His provision. He continues to faithfully reveal areas within our personal

---

[h] Genesis 3:17, 18

61

lives that have been affected by our broken world. We refer to this process as sanctification, and the ongoing nature of sanctification shines a spotlight on the fact that all of us still have traces of poverty needing to be dealt with.

But why does all this matter? Before we begin trying to help those we regard as poor, it is vitally important to come to grips with the poverty we have in our own lives. We should not attempt to help others from a position of superiority, but rather meet them as fellow impoverished humans. We come, not only to assist them in their poverty, but also to let them expose our own. It is vital to understand this if we want to effectively help others.

A Comprehensive Cure ⑧

Once we realize that poverty is anything less than God's original design, we find traces of it almost everywhere. It exists in every nation, every government, and every culture. Poverty even lurks in our churches and hearts at times. Poverty is a comprehensive problem. But thankfully, God's antidote for this poverty is comprehensive as well. Those of us who have found salvation through the blood of Jesus Christ know that His sacrifice and teachings are the cure to this wide-ranging disease. As believers we all say we believe this. It is the right thing to say. But do you really believe that Jesus is the answer to all forms of poverty?

In their book *When Helping Hurts,* Steve Corbett and Brian Fikkert tell how they asked thousands of Christians why Jesus came to earth. They reported that in response to this question, "The vast majority of people say something like 'Jesus came to die on the cross to save us from our sins so that we can go to heaven.' "[1]

In other words, Jesus came to cure the poverty of relationship between God and me. While this is certainly true, if we view this answer as all-encompassing, it is a very narrow view of Christ's mission.

When Jesus was asked to read in the synagogue in Nazareth, He read from Isaiah's prophecy and then said, "This day is this scripture fulfilled in your ears."[a] In other words, He had just read His mission statement. This is why He came to earth. But notice the words Jesus read to them.

"The Spirit of the Lord is upon me, because he hath anointed me to preach the gospel to the poor; he hath sent me to heal the broken hearted, to preach deliverance to the captives, and recovering of sight to the blind, and to set at liberty them that are bruised, to preach the

---

[a] Luke 4:21

acceptable year of the Lord."[b]

Notice the comprehensiveness of Jesus' mission statement. Jesus was attaching Himself not only to this passage, but also to every promise given in the Old Testament regarding the coming King. He wasn't just on a mission to take men to heaven. Jesus came to relieve every ailment and every type of poverty that Adam's sin had placed upon men. He brought a comprehensive cure.

What does this mean? Will the follower of Jesus not have crop failure, sickness in the family, or financial difficulties? No, as I read accounts of the early followers of Jesus, it seems they had more troubles than the average citizen, not less. One of their Roman detractors said most of the early Christians were "in want, are cold, are laboring in hard work and hunger . . ."[2] And yet, as those believers allowed the power of God to work in their lives, each difficulty became an avenue to demonstrate to a lost world the redeeming power of God. Each struggle gave opportunity. The early Christians were able to take the worst this cursed world could throw at them and use it to demonstrate the power of the Gospel.

This is still happening. I still see followers of Jesus redeeming the effects of the curse and using difficulties as open doors. They are providing relief after disasters, teaching better farming techniques, praying with the sick, and walking beside those with financial problems. Jesus sacrificed willingly to help people with their natural afflictions and problems, and His followers do the same. It is part of God's comprehensive redemption and cure.

As we reach out to others with the Gospel of Jesus Christ, it is important to offer all that Christ brought to bless mankind. Recently I received a call from a congregation that has planted several churches in developing countries. These men talked of their original vision and some of the challenges they have faced along the way. The churches they have planted are growing, and many have been blessed by their endeavors. But recently they have experienced difficulty.

"We started out," one of them told me, "with a vision to focus only on spiritual need." They had heard many stories of missions that had become bogged down with humanitarian aid. They wanted to avoid

[b] Luke 4:18, 19

the problems of dependency that can accompany these efforts, so to avoid those problems, they decided to focus only on spiritual need and try to ignore the physical.

The person explained more. "But as time went on, their natural needs became too great to ignore. How can you disregard such extreme poverty? How can you preach Jesus and ignore empty stomachs?" They realized such a scenario wasn't possible, so they decided to start providing small amounts of natural help when the need was great. But since humanitarian aid wasn't their primary vision, they spent little time analyzing how they administered it. It is always easier to alleviate symptoms rather than work on the root cause, and that's exactly what this mission did. Several years passed, and by the time we talked, that mission was in trouble. Every day there was a steady and growing stream of people coming to their mission asking for food and other aid, and the mission realized they were turning the people into beggars.

Notice what instigated their dilemma. These believers had assumed they could separate the Gospel from the physical needs—that somehow they could offer a cure for people's relationship with God without addressing material poverty, which was ravaging the community. This scenario has become all too common in impoverished nations. Where does the idea come from that we can offer spiritual help but ignore the natural? Certainly not from the life and example of Jesus!

We find Jesus going about doing good, healing the sick, and curing all manner of natural diseases. We even find Him producing bread and fish to feed the hungry who came to listen to Him. Jesus didn't ignore the natural. But neither did He make it His primary focus. It was just one part of His comprehensive cure.

What about the teaching and example of the apostles? In all of Christian history and mission work, we surely would not find anyone more valuable to the cause or more zealous in spreading the Gospel than the Apostle Paul. His time was valuable at this time when the message was still new and the mission field wide open, and there was not a minute to lose. But notice the instructions Paul said he received from Peter, James, and John as they sent him out: "Only they would that we should remember the poor; the same which I also was forward to do."[c]

Remember the Poor?

Here was a man called specifically as a messenger to the heathen, a man who had just received special revelations from God and was able to speak, write, and explain great theological truths. Why did the other apostles remind Paul to remember the poor as he went? Perhaps the reminder was merely because we all tend to forget.

In our eagerness to share the spiritual power of the Gospel, it is possible to forget the poor. David Bercot, commenting on this tendency in *The Kingdom That Turned the World Upside Down*, said, "I find it so strange that among Bible-believing Christians, serving the poor is typically viewed as a second-class ministry. If you're not out saving souls, then many consider your ministry to be essentially valueless."[3]

The teachings of Jesus and the example of the apostles are clear. Reaching out to the poor must be an integral part of our ministry. It is not an enemy to Christ's Gospel, but rather a part of it. Paul said that God has "given to us the ministry of reconciliation."[d] That word *reconciliation* can also be translated as "restoration." As disciples of Jesus Christ, we are called to join His work of restoration, to free men holistically from the grip of the curse. As Isaac Watts said many years ago, "He comes to make His blessings flow, far as the curse is found!"

Needed Balance

Great care must be taken with this focus as well. There is a segment of modern "Christianity" that puts undue emphasis on restoring our material world. We often refer to this teaching as the health and wealth gospel. Teachers within these groups tend to focus on one's relationship with material resources and how to create wealth and pursue materialistic

[c] Galatians 2:10

[d] 2 Corinthians 5:18

goals. Wealth, they teach, is simply a sign of God's blessing and should be pursued. Needless to say, this is a heretical and improper view of the Gospel. While part of Jesus' ministry was to meet physical or natural needs, to promote this as the primary focus of the Gospel would be as improper as neglecting it altogether.

To What Purpose
As we remind ourselves of the importance of sharing a complete Gospel, it is important to also remember the ultimate purpose. God's will is that all men "be saved and come unto the knowledge of the truth."[e] God did not call us to be ministers of reconciliation just to make the world a nicer place to live. We are workers together with God as He continues the work of reconciling the world unto Himself.[f]

Several years ago I was visiting some believers in a very poor part of Central America. We talked at length about this issue of trying to separate the physical from the spiritual, and one brother made this observation: "I don't know of one person who has come to Christ here because of our medical clinic." He pointed up the road toward the clinic. "But it has demonstrated our care for them like nothing else could have. In fact, without it we probably wouldn't even have a church here."

Several vibrant churches are still in that area, and they continue to grow. The clinic demonstrates to the community what many of the works of Jesus did to the people in His day—love and reconciliation. That clinic gives context to the Gospel message and makes it believable.

Conclusion
The familiar Biblical account of the two men on the road to Emmaus always inspires me. The story begins with two downcast men moping along the path, and it ends with an all-out sprint back to Jerusalem to share the exciting news. But we must note a phrase in this account. As Jesus walked with the men and asked why they were so sad, they began to unburden their hearts. They told about their Lord, who they thought was gone forever, and described His life among them by saying, "Jesus of Nazareth, which was a prophet mighty in deed and word before God

[e] 1 Timothy 2:4
[f] 2 Corinthians 5:19

and all the people."[g] Consider this phrase, "mighty in deed and word." This little description encapsulates Christ's comprehensive Gospel and tells us what effective, redemptive ministry looks like.

Jesus didn't just walk around town sharing wonderful spiritual truths. He brought more than mere words. Neither did He go up and down the streets merely fixing all the physical ailments or passing out bread. His Gospel was more than just deeds. His was a Gospel of both words and deeds. It was a complete and comprehensive cure. Too often we try to separate word from deed and pit one against the other. But when united in a common purpose, each can complement the other and point a hurting world toward Jesus Christ more effectively than either could have accomplished alone.

---

[g] Luke 24:19

The Poor, the Lost, and the Heart of God (9)

We finished another delicious Sunday dinner followed by wonderful dessert, and as we sipped our coffee, the conversation shifted to a recent event that had made headlines. A tropical storm had hit a very poor country and left a path of destruction and misery in its wake. This country had been plagued with persistent poverty for years, and this storm on top of previous struggles seemed devastating. As we discussed the predicament, our discussion turned to the ongoing poverty prevalent in so many countries. One of the older men commented, "It is my opinion that anywhere you go on this globe, if a man is willing to work, he can make a good living. Poverty is simply a result of laziness and poor planning."

I was young at the time and didn't enter the conversation, but this comment stuck with me. They are poor because of laziness and poor planning. Really? Just a small percentage of the people on this globe are hardworking and diligent, and for some strange reason almost all of them happen to live in a handful of countries?

This all-encompassing remark was made by an individual who had never traveled beyond the boundaries of the United States, had lived all his life on the Midwestern farm he inherited when his father died, and was now quite prosperous even by American standards. His worldview had developed through a small window, yet he was positive he had a good grasp on worldwide poverty and its causes.

But reality is much different. There are many countries where people work much harder than most of us, yet continue to languish in material poverty. Past colonialism may be part of the problem in some of these countries. A powerful country overthrows a weaker one, exploits its natural resources, kills off those with management abilities, and eventually leaves. History records many situations like this. The departing power leaves a country with no governmental stability, insufficient infrastructure, and little ability to recover on its own. This is but one of many factors in countries that languish, and it is too simplistic to assume that people are poor only because of laziness. The cause of poverty is not that simple.

Essentially this man was saying that the poor are poor by choice. Consequently, we are wealthy because of wise decisions and a good work ethic. And of course, since this is true, we have little obligation to help—or so the reasoning goes.

So what is our obligation to the materially and spiritually poor? Do we have any responsibility to the occasional cries we hear coming from the other side of the wall?

Ralph Waldo Emerson once said, "Do not tell me, as a good man did today, of my obligation to put all poor men in good situations. Are they my poor?"[1] In other words, am I really responsible for poverty in the world today? When I go into the local Walmart and purchase items I know are inexpensive solely because the producers are people working in miserable sweatshops in other countries, am I partly to blame for global poverty? If coffee plantations offered American-level wages to the men, women, and children working on their farms, few of us could afford to drink it. By drinking coffee, am I contributing to global poverty?

Many groups out there try to persuade us that capitalism and wealthy, developed nations are responsible for the plight of the poor. But those who praise socialism and communism generally neglect to note that the poor usually do much worse under either of those systems. Capitalism can lead to exploiting the poor, but many have found communism and socialism much more oppressive. The cause of poverty is not just inferior government structures. The root cause of poverty is sin. And as long as sinful men control governments, we will have inequitable government structures and poverty. So are we, who live in wealthy nations, responsible for the world's poverty?

Responsible *For* Versus Responsible *To*

Buying inexpensive products and drinking coffee produced using inexpensive labor is not contributing to world hunger. In fact, if the developed countries suddenly stopped consuming coffee and other imported goods, many developing countries would experience economic disaster. Millions of workers who depend on these low-paying jobs for survival would immediately be out of work. Does that then free us to eat, drink, and be merry while we ignore the poor, since they aren't really our responsibility? No. Even though we cannot be blamed for their poverty, we are responsible. As one writer said, "I may not be responsible for the existence of world hunger. But I am responsible to do what I can to relieve it."[2]

I remember a discussion some years ago regarding how much we should focus on the poor. The topic was batted around from several angles, and one brother in particular forcefully argued that this focus of helping the poor, especially in other countries, was getting out of hand. He didn't see the logic in traveling to other countries and getting involved in projects to help alleviate poverty. But another brother there that night didn't say much. He just quietly sat there and listened to the debate.

After much discussion we went to bed. The next morning when we sat down for breakfast, the brother who hadn't said much the previous evening asked whether we could read Isaiah 58. The religious people of Isaiah's day were seeking God daily, delighting to know God, and placing much emphasis on fasting. They were making a great attempt to appear contrite before God in fasting, but God said, "Is not this the fast I have chosen? To loose the bands of wickedness, to undo the heavy burdens, and to let the oppressed go free, and that ye break every yoke? Is it not to deal thy bread to the hungry, and that thou bring the poor that are cast out to thy house? When thou seest the naked, that thou cover him; and that thou hide not thyself from thine own flesh?"[a]

We finished reading that morning and sat there in silence for a moment. Then the brother who had listened quietly the night before

---

[a] Isaiah 58:6, 7

said, "After the discussion last night, I didn't sleep very well. My mind kept coming back to this chapter. I don't know what all this chapter may be saying, but if we are going to debate about reaching out to the poor, regardless where they live, I don't want to be on the side that is discouraging it."

The Bible is clear regarding God's heart for the lost and the poor. Not only has God gone to great lengths in the past to reconcile the world to Himself, He is still very interested in the ongoing work of reconciliation. The follower of Jesus doesn't reach out to the materially and spiritually poor due to fear or in hope of reward. He does it because he is following and imitating Jesus.

A news reporter once observed Mother Teresa working in the slums of Calcutta. She was cleaning the wounds of a roadside leper. The reporter standing by, overcome by the filthy living conditions, blurted out, "I wouldn't do that for a million dollars!"

Mother Teresa replied, "Neither would I, but I would gladly do it for Christ."[3] I am challenged by this Catholic nun's example of following Jesus. Do I have that kind of passion for following Jesus? Am I as committed to loving and serving the poor as Jesus was?

But I Say Unto You . . .

After studying the Old Testament, we notice some major shifts when crossing into the New Testament. In the Old Testament, God had told His people to go into certain heathen countries and kill everyone—men, women, children, and even the livestock. But when Jesus appeared in the New Testament, He said that not only shouldn't we kill our enemies, but we are to love them!

In the Old Testament, allowance was made for a man to divorce his wife. In the new dispensation, marriage vows are binding for life. The old system had taught "an eye for an eye and a tooth for a tooth." But Jesus said things were changing. His followers were not to do violence to anyone—ever!

All these dramatic changes must have been difficult for the Jewish people. They had grown accustomed to a system that seemed fair and equitable. Suddenly Jesus presented a different paradigm that was difficult for these people to understand and digest. But amid all these revolutionary changes, something remained unmoved—God's love and concern for the lost and the poor.

From the beginning of His ministry, we see Jesus' words deal with the poor and God's intent for them. Blessing after blessing is proclaimed upon those whom we would call the unfortunate in society—the hurting, the mourning, the poor, the hungry, and the hated.[b] These words describe conditions and circumstances in life that most of us try to avoid. Yet obviously, even though some things are radically different in this new Kingdom, one aspect of it is still the same. God still has a heart for the poor and the lost!

But let's take this concept one step further. Anyone filled by the indwelling Christ will love what God loves. This truth is unavoidable. Notice these words of the Apostle John: "But whoso hath this world's good, and seeth his brother have need, and shutteth up his bowels of compassion from him, how dwelleth the love of God in him?"[c]

I have heard this verse dissected and analyzed by well-meaning believers, and generally the discussion revolves around what is meant by the word *brother*. Was John saying our obligation is only to other believers, or even exclusively to those in our own denomination?

> *If God would pour out His love only on those who deserve it, all of us would be in trouble.*

But as I listen to this question of who is my brother, I am reminded of another question presented to Jesus. "Who is my neighbor?"[d] asked a man who, Luke says, was trying to define the parameters. He wanted to know just what he had to do and what his obligations were.

But we can easily miss the point the Apostle John wants us to get. The message is very simple. If God dwells in us, we won't shut off our compassion! We won't sit around trying to define who we are obliged

[b] Luke 6:20-25
[c] 1 John 3:17
[d] Luke 10:29

to help. If God would pour out His love only on those who deserve it, all of us would be in trouble. God blessed us who are undeserving, and if His love dwells in us, we will have that same desire to reach out to the undeserving poor and lost.

Conclusion

From the beginning of the church in Acts, faithful followers of the Lord Jesus have put an emphasis on the poor. Many of them voluntarily lived in poverty to enable more giving. Clement of Alexandria said, "It is monstrous for one to live in luxury, while many are in want."[4] Clement recognized the utter foolishness of heaping wealth upon ourselves while claiming to imitate the life of Jesus.

Even unbelievers get uncomfortable when the gap gets too great. One of the first things most men do if they suddenly receive great wealth is to set up a foundation or some way of sharing with those who have less. Even those lepers way back in Elisha's day began to feel uncomfortable with that gap. They knew that the starving, naked, and miserable masses were just over that wall. Somehow that knowledge destroys some of the pleasure in plenty.

Sharing with those in need was interwoven throughout the Law, and this teaching continues through the New Testament as God reveals what He has in mind for His Kingdom.

John the Baptist arrived on the scene and said, "He that hath two coats, let him impart to him that hath none; and he that hath meat, let him do likewise."[e]

In the early part of His ministry, Jesus said, "Give to him that asketh of thee, and from him that would borrow of thee turn not thou away."[f]

One of the first items of business for the new church in Acts was to sell their goods and give to the poor.[g] One would have to either be blind or very eager to justify himself to miss God's desire for us. When you find within your heart a great burden and love for the lost and the poor, rejoice! God carries that same burden in His heart.

---

[e] Luke 3:11
[f] Matthew 5:42
[g] Acts 2:45

PART THREE

Unintended Consequences

Unintended Consequences

The idea had been discussed for hundreds of years. Various plans had been proposed, many countries had shown interest, and everyone agreed something needed to be done. What a blessing it would be for sailors and shipping companies alike if a shortcut could be found somewhere across Central America instead of needing to sail around the southern tip of South America. Cutting across this relatively small sliver of land would reduce the route between New York and San Francisco by about 18,000 miles. Various surveys were made between 1850 and 1875, and it was finally decided that a route across the area we know as Panama would be the most practical. Finally, after several attempts had failed, the French committed to this project of constructing a shipping canal in the early 1880s. The endeavor was led by Ferdinand Marie de Lesseps, the man who had successfully overseen the construction of the Suez Canal.

The Panama project was a colossal undertaking. There were mountains to cut through, political battles to be fought, and huge amounts of money to be raised. After a valiant attempt, the French eventually gave up around 1890. They moved out of the area, leaving behind an unfinished project, massive amounts of machinery, and many buildings they had constructed for the project. Obviously they had underestimated the magnitude of the project. Eventually the United States took up the work, although it wouldn't be until 1914 that all fifty miles of the Panama Canal would finally be completed.

Without question, the Panama Canal project was one of the most massive, difficult, and spectacular engineering feats in the history of mankind. Thousands of men, working in a harsh and foreign environment, poured themselves into the work, many at the cost of their own lives. In fact, it is estimated that over 27,000 men died in the endeavor.[1] Dangerous working conditions, rock avalanches, and rain-induced mudslides made the project extremely hazardous. But two other foes claimed more lives than all the other hazards put together: yellow fever and malaria.

Thousands of men died after becoming infected with these dreaded diseases, and these two enemies alone repeatedly threatened to bring the entire project to a halt. We must remember that when this project began, the medical community was not yet aware that mosquitoes carried these diseases. While the cause was still unknown, various theories and notions floated around the medical community. The word *malaria* itself stems from the Italian words *mala aria,* meaning "bad air," and the prevalent belief for years was that the disease was simply caused by the misty jungle nights. During the early years of the project, as men became infected, the French constructed a hospital that was operated by a religious order, the French Sisters of Charity.

While these women had little medical training, they were religiously devoted to the cause and did the best they could. Every night they would carefully close all the doors and windows in an attempt to keep out those dangerous night mists purported to carry malaria. But in the morning when they returned, they repeatedly found patients in worse condition or even dead. It was discouraging, and they felt overwhelmed. This dreaded disease, they believed, was stealthily creeping in through the cracks each night while they were asleep.

But others weren't so sure. They were doing a good job of shutting out the night air, yet the problem wasn't going away. What was the real cause? And then someone mentioned the ants. These little creatures could be seen snaking across the hospital floor and even up the legs of the beds. As nurses found these ants in hospital beds, they began to suspect that these little critters were actually the culprits.

The evidence seemed convincing, so they began discussing how these malaria-carrying ants could be stopped. Finally someone proposed an apparently brilliant solution. What if the legs of each bed were placed in pans of water?[2] Since ants avoid water, this would effectively stop them from traveling up the bed frames and into the beds. This plan was embraced by all and quickly put into action. Leg by leg, each bed was lifted and placed in a pan of standing water. We can imagine the thrill those nurses experienced as they gleefully watched the little ants approach these formidable pans of water and turn back. The foe had been defeated!

Yet the dying continued. Even though the beds were now ant free, the scourge of malaria marched on. In fact, it seemed to be claiming even more of their patients than it had before. Finally, in 1897, Ronald Ross successfully demonstrated that malaria was transferred, not by ants or by damp night air, but by the lowly mosquito.[3] And all those pans of water under each hospital bed, though placed there with the greatest intentions, were not helping the cause.

Even worse, imagine how these diligent and hardworking nurses must have felt when they discovered the awful truth. Not only did those pans of water not help the cause, they actually did incredible damage. Mosquitoes need standing water to breed, and in these pans, mosquitoes found the very environment they needed to multiply. These nurses had quite unknowingly placed the cause of death at each corner of the patients' beds. All their efforts, though intended to fight this dreaded disease, had instead created a deadly environment where malaria could thrive. Their actions, meant for good, had been extremely detrimental.

More Than Good Motives

We don't live long before discovering the reality of unintended consequences. We are not always good fixers. We respond to one problem, only to discover we have created another. Our motives may be good and our efforts valiant, yet we find the actual results much different than we expected. And unfortunately, many times we see the scourge of unintended consequences in our attempts to help those in need.

We have looked at the power of sin in our world and the comprehensive power of Jesus Christ to reconcile and make things right. But we must also come to grips with the realization that not all of our attempts to help are actually helpful. Sometimes our efforts to assist others turn out to be a detriment to the very people we were trying to help. Like the French Sisters of Charity during the construction of the Panama Canal, our motives are good. Yet we find ourselves harming the very people we mean to help.

Several years ago I was involved in a small building project in Haiti. We had been going to Haiti with various people who wanted to help, and as we began to understand the people and the culture, we saw that some methods of helping worked better than others. We also discovered that some ways of doing things didn't work at all. So after several years of working on these projects, a couple of us put together a small manual to help initiate newcomers. Some had never visited a developing country, so we warned them about food diseases, tried to prepare them for culture shock, and warned them against giving too many handouts. In addition to asking each team member to read this little handbook before they traveled, we also had some discussions once we arrived to help initiate those less familiar with the situation.

But it seemed no matter how much was said or written, people who had never visited a developing country before had difficulty understanding why giving too freely might be a detriment to their new Haitian friends. After all, we obviously have too much and they have so little. What could be wrong with unloading some of our surplus on them? I noticed that many times in our discussions, those who had never visited before would become defensive. How could it harm to give these poor people things they obviously needed? So to avoid the potential problems we knew could develop, we asked team members to keep any gifts they had brought until the project was complete. At that point we would work through a trusted Haitian and try to bless the nationals with shoes, clothes, or school supplies they obviously lacked.

Most team members were very understanding. But I still vividly remember one older team member who arrived at a project site for the first time. He had been traveling for a few hours and obviously felt overwhelmed by the many unusual sights along the way. Our project was in a very poor area, and as he stepped off the truck and looked around at a level of poverty he probably never knew existed, he immediately forgot all he had been told. He had a compassionate heart, and within a matter of minutes had given away almost everything he had brought with him, including his extra clothes. He just instantly liquidated. His heart was so touched he gave all he had. But as a result, the next two weeks were miserable. Every time he poked his head out of his tent, he was instantly swarmed. Instead of being just another worker on a community project, he suddenly became the wealthy American, the bearer of gifts. Toward the end of his trip, some of the locals even became a little hostile. After all, he was obviously wealthy and they had great need. Why couldn't he just keep on giving as he had at first?

Effectively blessing others, whether in our local congregations or in foreign countries, calls for prayerful discernment. It requires more than just good motives and a desire to help. There is no question in my mind that this man had pure motives. But he painfully discovered that good motives alone don't always ensure good results. There is also a great need for prayerful, godly discernment.

Conclusion

The French Sisters of Charity in Panama really wanted to bless the men suffering from malaria, and we don't doubt their intentions. People don't leave their homes, travel to the jungles of Panama, and risk their lives without good reason. But good intentions and self-sacrifice were not enough. Only as they continued to investigate, listen to others, and finally admit they had made mistakes, were they able to win the battle against malaria.

Sometimes in our attempts to help, we can become so worried about hurting the people we are trying to help that we succumb to fear. We see all the unintended consequences of other attempts to alleviate poverty, and we fear that our attempts may also do damage. But ignoring the suffering because of fear is not an option for the believer. Paul told Timothy, "God hath not given us the spirit of fear; but of power, and of love, and of a sound mind."[a] I think of this verse often when working with those in need.

Helping the poor isn't always as easy as it first appears. We need to continually look to God for power and make sure we operate with love.

---

[a] 2 Timothy 1:7

But we also need to use the sound mind God has given us. If we want to effectively help, we need to occasionally stop, analyze the results of our efforts, humbly admit our failures, and prayerfully use the sound mind God gave us to plot a better course.

Searching Out the Cause

O n March 21, 2009, *The Wall Street Journal* published an article entitled "Why Foreign Aid Is Hurting Africa." This article explored the painful reality of ongoing aid to impoverished countries in our world. "Over the past 60 years," it said, "at least $1 trillion of development-related aid has been transferred from rich countries to Africa. Yet real per-capita income today is lower than it was in the 1970s, and more than 50 percent of the population—over 350 million people—live on less than a dollar a day, a figure that has nearly doubled in two decades."[1]

Even though a massive amount of money has surged into many of these extremely poor countries, the results have not always been good. This writing highlights the fact that many countries are even poorer now than before. In fact, many of the countries that have received the most are doing the worst. The article, written by an author who grew up in Zambia, provided this story to illustrate why much of the aid has proved ineffective in his country.

A mosquito net maker in an African town manufactured five hundred mosquito nets each week and employed ten men from town. In Africa, the average employee supports at least fifteen people, so this little factory was providing an income for around 150 citizens in this town. Demand was great for mosquito nets. Malaria was a problem there, so this small business was always busy producing and selling mosquito nets. In fact, they couldn't keep up with the demand.

One day a Western aid organization rolled in to assess the situation in this impoverished African town. They had heard malaria was a problem there, and of course, they knew malaria is transferred through mosquitoes. Wanting to help, they called back to their headquarters and asked for a shipment of mosquito nets. Within a few months the organization returned with a shipment of 100,000 mosquito nets, which it generously distributed free of charge among the locals. After taking pictures to show how they helped these people, the aid organization returned home.

Actual Results

But let's go back to this African town. What was the long-term result? And how did this affect the little mosquito net factory? They couldn't sell mosquito nets while others gave the same item away free. This little factory was soon out of business and its ten workers unemployed. Consequently, the 150 citizens supported by those jobs lost their income.

But the article went on to analyze the impact on the rest of the town. Mosquito nets don't last forever, and in a few years many of the free nets would be torn and useless. Who would replace these nets? How would this town defend itself in the future against mosquitoes and malaria? We could argue that this African town is now worse off than before. Not only do they have fewer jobs, but they have probably lost their ability to replace damaged nets. And as a result, future entrepreneurs will be slow to risk their capital and energy in starting up a new factory for fear this scenario might happen again.

One danger of recounting this illustration is that someone may conclude these countries don't need help, or that providing aid only creates more problems. But the article was not written so that we ignore the plight of the poor. In fact, its message was just the opposite. If we are going to effectively help those on the other side of the wall, we need to give more thought to root causes instead of focusing solely on the immediate, visible need. This will require *more* effort and attention—not less.

A Message From Job

In the book of Job, we see Job's friends confronting him and accusing his character. Each time, Job provided a defense, including one phrase that captures a powerful thought. Job's friends had accused him of neglecting the poor, and Job responded by saying, "I was a father to the poor: and the cause which I knew not I searched out."[a]

Job didn't just deal with symptoms created by material poverty. He tried to investigate and find the cause. He was willing to ask some questions. He wanted to find out what was really going on. Too often we respond to perceived need without asking any questions.

Consider this on a local level. Imagine you have a brother in your congregation who continually has trouble with credit card debt. Each time he gets behind on his payments, he comes to you and asks for help. Month after month he lands on your doorstep needing just a little cash to make his minimum payment. You don't see any major crisis in his life, yet he falls just a little short each

> *Too often we respond to perceived need without asking any questions.*

month. Are you blessing that brother if you continue to make his monthly payments for him? Isn't investigating the cause simply part of showing brotherly love? Wouldn't it be prudent to ask some questions?

Of course it would. Just dealing with the symptom by making his payments could harm him and might keep him from confronting the root cause of his poverty. But sometimes what is so clear to us in a local setting can be difficult to understand where extreme poverty exists. But the same principles do apply. We need to take the time, as Job said, to search out the cause.

Just a Few Questions

Let's go back to our story about the mosquito net factory. What could the aid organization have done? How could they have averted the tragic ending to this story? The answer is simple. They could have asked a few questions.

What would have happened if they would have first spent some time learning from the local citizens? These people were not ignorant of the problem. They understood that mosquitoes carry malaria and that mosquito nets greatly aid its prevention. And they had some valuable information. One of the locals might have said, "Hey, there is a

---

[a] Job 29:16

mosquito net factory right here in town. You don't need to ship nets halfway around the world. We make them here!"

If this organization had visited the factory and asked more questions, they might have found the factory wasn't able to keep up with demand due to older equipment or lack of capital. Maybe, instead of shipping in a container of nets, they could have provided a small loan to update the equipment, hire additional help, and consequently assist both the health and the long-term vitality of this community. But they failed to take time to fully investigate.

Several years ago while our family was traveling along Interstate 5 in northern California, we stopped at a rest area. As we got out of our vehicle, a woman walked up and started telling us her story. She had been traveling with her sister to a funeral, she claimed, and their van had broken down. They had used all their money to have it repaired, and now they didn't have any money for food. She wondered if we would give them some money to buy food.

I was skeptical of her story since others had approached us like this at rest areas numerous times. For some reason there was always a funeral or some other tear-jerking story, and a need for either fuel or food. So I told this woman I wouldn't give her cash but that we did have some apples in our vehicle that they could have. She apologized profusely and said they wouldn't want to take our food (somehow taking our money didn't bother her), but I insisted and took some apples over to her vehicle. When she opened the back of her van, it was loaded with food. Obviously others had already given them a great deal of food, and her reluctance to take mine was explained. She stood there with a red face while I unloaded my apples on top of a pile of apples she already had. I gave her some exhortation about honesty, and we proceeded on our trip. So often we are in a hurry and don't feel we have time to fully probe the situation (which is why beggars linger at rest stops). But if our goal is to really help the person, we should take time to investigate whenever possible.

Keep Asking Questions
Not only should we investigate *before* helping individuals and

communities, but it is also extremely important to keep asking questions *after* giving help. Going back to the mosquito net story, let's follow this aid organization as they go back to their headquarters. They return home with an abundance of pictures showing needy people lined up, gratefully receiving free mosquito nets. These photos end up in a brochure telling donors how they helped this impoverished African village. But did anyone ever go back to investigate how this aid really impacted the town? Was the goal to make happy donors or to actually provide aid to the poor? And what about the donors? Shouldn't they have been asking questions? Did anyone really hold this organization accountable?

> *God's heart has never been to just take care of symptoms.*

Conclusion

God's heart has never been to just take care of symptoms. The reconciling power of Jesus Christ is intended, as the writer of Hebrews says, "to save them to the uttermost."[b] God wants to do more than just make things look better on the outside. He is interested in exposing root causes and bringing transformation. God works with the heart because He knows that until the heart is changed, the symptoms keep reoccurring. As one author said, "At the heart of every problem is a problem of the heart."[2]

This also proves true when dealing with people living in ongoing poverty. It is much easier to give a poor man a small gift, take a nice picture, and send him on his way than to take time to investigate the underlying cause. When you meet that beggar along the street, the easiest thing is to give him a little cash and hurry on. It is harder and requires much more time to investigate and deal with root causes. The brother having difficulty with credit card debt probably does not have a money problem as much as a management problem. But it is imperative to ask questions and search out the root cause of the visible symptom if we are going to help him in a meaningful way.

---

[b] Hebrews 7:25

Wealth and Wisdom (12)

Born in India, Girdharilal Maurya[1] works day after day making and selling leather products in his village. Working with animal skins is an occupation looked down on by most in India, but Girdharilal is one of 160 million born into the Untouchable or Dalit caste, and he is destined to a life of hard work and grinding poverty. The very fact that he was born into this particular caste is proof to others within the community that he deserves his life of poverty. Why else would he be born into the Untouchables, if not to pay for sins in a previous life? But Girdharilal worked hard and managed well; consequently his business prospered. People liked the quality of his products and his sales increased. Using the profits, Girdharilal purchased a small plot of land just outside his village. This caused no small stir within his village. Had he forgotten he was an Untouchable? What right did an Untouchable have to improve his life? But it was when he asked to use the village well that his neighbors decided this was enough. Who did he think he was, trying to rise above his caste by purchasing property and asking to use water from the public well? From his neighbors' perspective, Girdharilal needed to learn a lesson.

One night while Girdharilal was away in a nearby city, eight men from a higher caste came to his little farm. They broke down his fences, took his tractor, beat his wife and daughter, and burned down his house. The message to Girdharilal was clear: stay at the bottom where you belong!

While we have trouble connecting with this mindset, for many this is quite normal. If you are born into a Hindu family in India, you automatically enter the caste system, one of the world's longest surviving forms of social stratification. It follows a basic belief: men are not created equal.

While rural India may regard this as normal, in the developed world an opposite phenomenon occurs. Our culture likes the underdog. In America we have grown up admiring the rags-to-riches stories made famous by authors like Horatio Alger. Our culture likes the man who starts with nothing, works hard, uses his head, and finally becomes financially successful.

From our youngest years we have heard the famous mantra attributed to Ben Franklin, "Early to bed and early to rise, makes a man healthy, wealthy, and wise." This saying encapsulates a thought diametrically opposed to what is believed in India. In our capitalistic culture, we are all born equal. The man who makes good choices succeeds, becomes wealthy, and is deemed wise. In India, the caste a person is born into determines how high he may rise. Regardless how intelligent or how many natural abilities he may have, in their culture he is defined by his caste.

We shake our heads in bewilderment at the Indian caste system. Why should the family a man is born into define his future? What an illogical and problematic system! But we need to humbly conclude that our system also has some inherent problems. There are negative consequences when we assume the wealthy are also wise. Let's look at some subtle negative effects of equating wealth with wisdom.

- **"I have earned it!"** Sometimes we refer to a wealthy person as a self-made man. The tendency, seen in the life of Nebuchadnezzar, is to ascribe all you have been blessed with to your own resourcefulness, ability, and wisdom. The Apostle Paul takes aim at this assumption in the church at Corinth when he says, "For who maketh thee to differ from another? And what has thou that thou didst not receive?"[a] Even if your choices and wisdom did help create your wealth, who gave you the intellect? Who provided an economy that rewarded those wise decisions? Who gave you the natural resources to build wealth? In reality, all of us come into the world with nothing, and anything we have while on the earth is simply a blessing from God.

[a] 1 Corinthians 4:7

- **Appearing wealthy makes one appear wise.** If a young man listens to the older ones talk in our culture, he soon learns how to appear wise. All he has to do is purchase the things the wealthy surround themselves with. Go ahead and buy that new car, remodel the house, purchase the latest technology, and buy those fine clothes. These items inform observers that you are wealthy. You can accomplish all this in our culture by using debt, and those looking on might assume that because you look wealthy, you must also be wise. Some of our young families, and at times those who aren't so young, get sucked into this materialistic mindset by using this logic. This tendency is a dangerous byproduct of equating wealth and wisdom.

- **Material wealth equals spiritual wisdom.** Once we subconsciously decide that tangible wealth is an indicator of a man's natural ability and wisdom, it is only a small jump to conclude that wealth indicates spiritual wisdom as well. If you look into our conservative churches, you will often find that those selected to fill roles of spiritual leadership are also comparatively wealthy. We have difficulty remembering the two are not always synonymous. Peering into the early church, we get a different picture. Early leaders like Cyprian were known, not for having wealth, but for giving it up. Cyprian was converted to the Christian faith at the age of forty. He was wealthy, but when he found the Lord, he liquidated his entire estate, giving it to the poor. He didn't want an abundance of material possessions to hamper his walk with God. The church at Carthage viewed this as a sign of commitment to Jesus, and Cyprian was selected as a bishop of their church at a relatively young age. They did not see material wealth as a sign of great wisdom, but as a potential snare and a fetter.

- **We assume we have nothing to learn from those with fewer resources.** We would never want to identify with a caste system like they have in India. Yet how many times do we feel superior in intelligence simply because we have a better checking account balance? Is that any less ridiculous? In India the upper castes believe the poor are deprived because they have sinned in a previous life. In our setting we come to believe the poor must experience poverty because they lack wisdom. Sometimes the materially poor do use poor methods. But many of us make better life choices, not because of greater intelligence, but because we have been surrounded by good role models and teachers. Wealth is not always an indicator of intelligence or wisdom.

Several years ago I came face to face with my tendency to equate wealth and wisdom. I stood in the middle of a poor city in a foreign country, watching people at their daily tasks. I began to ponder how I would fare if someone would suddenly drop me into this setting. I pictured myself abruptly thrust into their daily life, forced to deal with their mode of transportation and the challenges they face. Would I survive? No. I would probably starve if they didn't help me! I didn't know how to prepare their food or get clean water, and I didn't know the language. If someone dropped me off here, I would instantly be at the mercy of the locals.

> *If I couldn't even take care of myself, why did I think I could jump out of a Land Cruiser and instantly begin sharing advice about how they could improve their lives? After all, these people around me were alive. Something was working!*

I had come here to help these people, to teach, and to offer advice. I was supposed to have the answers, so it was humbling to admit that without their help, I probably couldn't even stay alive. Wasn't it rather presumptuous to assume I was qualified to immediately tell them what they should be doing? If I couldn't even take care of myself, why did I think I could jump out of a Land Cruiser and instantly begin sharing advice about how they could improve their lives? After all, these people around me were alive. Something was working!

The ugly reality is that I tend to equate wisdom with wealth. I have subconsciously assumed that because I was born into a wealthy culture and carry an American passport, I am wise. And though I might vehemently protest being labeled prejudiced or proud, many times these titles have been accurate. I have assumed that my material wealth indicates intelligence and wisdom.

Make no mistake, this doesn't mean the materially poor have nothing to learn. Many times they have an enormous need for teaching. And those of us coming from wealthy countries have an opportunity to bless people trying to survive in abject poverty. Basic business skills, work ethic, and spiritual understanding are lacking in these countries where poverty reigns. But to teach effectively, humility is essential. And though you may be called to teach, you will always have things to learn as well.

Helping at Home

This principle is just as valuable at home as abroad. Certain people in most congregations are good at business but have little time for interpersonal relationships. They like to make things happen. For this kind of person, sitting around trying to understand someone's heart doesn't feel like anything is happening. We could say he is long on production and short on relationships. Let's call this man Mr. Business.

But most of our congregations also have those who focus on relationships and try to understand what makes people tick. They can sit for hours and listen to the heart of a struggling individual. Sometimes this kind of person tends to be a poor manager or businessman. He is long on relationships and short on business, and we could refer to this man as Mr. Relationship.

When Mr. Relationship runs into financial trouble and needs someone to assist him, Mr. Business will probably get tapped. Obviously Mr. Business understands how things work, so he would be the logical choice to help Mr. Relationship. But we need to understand something. We have just seen that both Mr. Business and Mr. Relationship have strengths and weaknesses in their lives. All the money Mr. Business has in the bank doesn't make him good at relationships. Neither does Mr. Relationship's ability to assist people emotionally take care of the stack of unpaid bills on his desk. Both of them have something to learn from the other. If Mr. Business can humbly grasp this truth before he tries to help Mr. Relationship, he will find his advice more readily received. Both have something to offer, and both have something to learn.

This principle is true around the globe. All of us have something to learn from others. Regardless where you live or what you have learned, you can learn something from the person you are trying to help. None of us are exempt. One of our greatest hurdles in assisting others is really understanding and believing this fact. But if we try to learn, even when called to teach, our message will be better received and everyone will come away enriched. Some of my most valuable times of self-examination have come while working among the materially poor. But first I must humbly open my mind to the reality that I have something to learn from the poor.

Importance of Buy-In

There is another point so important we dare not miss it here. One of the major hurdles in helping the materially poor, especially in under-developed countries, is getting the local people to buy into the project. Many missions go into these countries with ambitious plans and development projects, only to find a few years later that little has changed. For some reason the local people didn't get behind the project, and consequently the effort had little value. Why?

In his book, *Giving Wisely?* Jonathan Martin tells of a well-meaning church group that traveled to Mexico to help a small indigenous congregation. This little church was located in a shantytown just outside Mexico City and was extremely poor. All of them, including the pastor, lived in makeshift plastic tents. The American congregation wanted to help, so they raised some funds, traveled to Mexico, and built a new church building for this impoverished congregation. They even built a nice little house for the pastor. After all, they reasoned, a man of God shouldn't have to live under a filthy scrap of plastic tarp.

This group of charitable Americans worked hard, and after they finished the project, they packed up their tools, hugged the Mexican believers they had come to love, and headed back north. For many of them, their lives would never be the same. They had seen a need, correctly realized they should share, and went to the rescue of this underprivileged church. Then they went home to show pictures of the project to their friends and talk about what a blessing it is to help those in need.

But little did these Americans know that shortly after their vehicles were out of sight, the church members disassembled the very building the Americans had just constructed. Reusing the materials, they rebuilt the building the way they really had wanted it and at the location they had wanted in the first place. But even worse was the long-term spiritual effect on the church. Just one year later this once-thriving church was almost totally dysfunctional.

How can this be? How could constructing a church building and a new home for the pastor destroy a church? Martin explains it in his book. "First, it raised the pastor to a level higher than those he ministered to, creating an artificial inequity. Second, the building wasn't a product of the locals' vision, giving, and hard work. In other words, it had nothing to do with them at all, but everything to do with America. It left the locals wondering, 'Whose church is this, anyway?' "[2]

Martin went on to say dissent broke out in the church because it looked like the pastor had sold out to the American ways and customs. There was suspicion he might even be receiving ongoing aid. Consequently, this once-flourishing church was torn apart in the resulting turmoil. They were worse off than if "help" had never come.

No one can doubt the sincerity or good intentions of the American church group. They really wanted to help these people. So what went wrong?

We who are wealthy desperately need to share, for the blinding effect of wealth is part of the root problem in this true story. We tend to equate affluence with intelligence, and the more wealth we have, the less we generally feel we need to ask questions. But what if these Americans would have first asked some questions? What if they had first gone to this little shantytown and taken the time to hear the needs and desires of these people? What if they had taken someone along who understood the culture they were entering? And what might have happened if they could have seen themselves as fellow learners in this fight against poverty?

These building projects can greatly bless a local congregation in an impoverished setting. But when we assume that wealth and wisdom are synonymous, we generally ask few questions. And when we fail to ask questions, we usually harm those we try to help.

Conclusion

Perhaps no example in Scripture exposes the folly of this belief like the church at Laodicea. Rich and increased with goods, they believed they had need of nothing, yet Jesus said they overlooked something. They had assumed they were rich, but Jesus said they were "wretched, and miserable, and poor, and blind, and naked."[b] They thought they were wise and could see clearly, but they actually had distorted vision and were not as wise as they thought.

Wealth blinds us. It subtly causes us to assume we see things clearly. But the truth is generally just the opposite. Paul told Timothy, "Charge them that are rich in this world, that they be not high minded . . ."[c]

Why did Paul give rich, "successful" Christians a negative warning like this? Wasn't it because material wealth can snare us, and we tend to believe we are wise when we are wealthy?

---

[b] Revelation 3:17
[c] 1 Timothy 6:17

The Problem of Paternalism

Several years ago I received a call from Dale. He had just returned from a trip to Mexico, and his head still swirled with all the new sights, smells, and impressions. Dale had never visited a foreign country before, so this trip made quite an impression. From a global perspective, Mexico isn't all that poor. In fact, considering all the countries based on their wealth per capita, Mexico is easily within the wealthier half of the world.[1] The majority of the world would love to experience their level of wealth. But if all you have ever known is middle class America, and your only reference point is our affluent culture, Mexico is poor indeed, especially if you get away from the major cities.

So Dale returned home with many thoughts and ideas. I listened as he described what he had observed in Mexico. He talked about unemployment and the need for improvement in their housing, transportation, and medical facilities. But then Dale went on to share his burden for their lack of sanitation.

"Gary," he said with great feeling, "there are entire villages down there where the people don't even have showers! Surely we could go down and install some showers for them." He described how some of us could take a load of plumbing supplies and improve their situation within a short time.

After Dale had talked about this great need for showers in Mexico and how we could easily fix this problem for some of them, I asked him how he would decide who to help. When you drive into a village and start your "shower installing ministry," who gets the showers?

For Dale this seemed easy. Of course he would begin with the believers who live there. After all, they are our brothers and sisters, and each of them should have a good shower! So we discussed the impact this might have on the village and even the local church. When you are giving out free showers to everyone who belongs to a little church, just how long do you think that church will remain small? Do we really want free showers to motivate church growth?

I suspect by the end of our conversation Dale viewed me as an uncaring and cold-hearted American. But this account illustrates two things that happen many times when we begin trying to "fix" another culture.

A Longer Wish List

First, we increase the length of their wish list. Was anyone in this village aware they needed showers? Likely, most of them had never even seen a shower, let alone wished for one. But just the act of going in and installing showers would have created longings they didn't have before we arrived.

When we arrive in a culture poorer than our own, we usually feel some guilt. When Dale stood under his nice warm shower at home, he probably thought about those poor Mexicans. And part of what drives us to improve the standard of living for the poor is guilt. This isn't all bad. Many of us do need to stop and ask ourselves if all the luxuries we surround ourselves with are really necessary. But introducing showers, which they didn't know they needed and probably wouldn't use, would merely show them how much they lack and increase their level of discontent.

A Shift in Focus

The second result of giving out free gifts to people living in abject poverty is that their focus begins to shift from their available resources to yours. Before you arrived, they viewed their soil, their abilities, their local markets, and their possessions as the primary resources for their community. When difficult situations arose, they probably talked about how they could meet and overcome each crisis using their available resources. But when you drive into a village in your new SUV and begin handing out gifts, their focus abruptly shifts from their resources to yours. Suddenly you become the target of their requests. You become the answer to all their needs and wants. After all, why hoe, plant, weed, and water when everything you need is available off the back of a truck? We gradually become like parents to them. This process is known as paternalism.

But this tendency isn't found only in foreign cultures. Many years ago I saw the same phenomenon occur in a local family that had many financial difficulties. People tried to help in various ways. When their car gave out, someone bought them another one. When they had medical bills, somehow the need was met. In some ways it was a beautiful sight, the body of Christ working together to help each member. But in spite of ever-increasing financial difficulties, the father in this home seemed to become less and less concerned. In fact, it became obvious that he expected others in the congregation to resolve each crisis as it came. The father began to view the church as a child would his parents. The child expects the parent to think for him, watch out for him, and take care of problems as they come.

Paternalism isn't a problem only because the ones providing aid begin to fill the role of parent. A worse side effect is that the ones receiving aid begin to act like children. The giver of aid does the thinking, watches for danger, and resolves problems. The receiver of aid sees little need to think creatively, search for solutions, or use his God-given ability to imagine possibilities. If this scenario continues long enough, he becomes even more helpless than before the aid arrived.

Eastern Europe today is an example of the long-term results of paternalism on a grand scale. For years the communist government played the role of parent. The people were given little incentive to work hard, and regardless how much effort the person put forth or how resourceful he was on the job, the pay stayed the same. Consequently, efficiency dropped dramatically and waste was rampant. Over time they simply lost their ability to work efficiently or think creatively.

Today you can drive past the remains of thousands of unsuccessful collective farms. They stand as a monument to the failed communistic policies of the past. But worse than the crumbling buildings are the millions of people left in the wake of that paternalistic mindset. For them, the communist government was like a parent, and they had become like children. Now that it is gone, they have floundered. Like orphaned children, they struggle to provide for themselves.

Recently I talked to a consultant who had traveled to Kazakhstan in the former Soviet Union to help a dairy find better food safety techniques. His project began in 2001, ten years after the fall of communism, yet the effects of paternalism lingered. It didn't take long to see that the workers hadn't been taught efficiency. The farm had 312 employees managing 383 cows! This farming operation had been developed under state rule years before, and now that change had come, they had no idea how to work as a free enterprise. For years they had been taught to never do more than was asked, and this inefficient mentality lingered. The consultant said they found those under the age of thirteen most receptive to learning a better way of life. For the older ones, change was hard. For too many years the government had acted like parents, and they had lost the ability to think and work efficiently. This problem still pervades much of Eastern Europe and the former Soviet Union. They have good soil and resources to provide for themselves, but the need for teaching and training remains great.

"I Don't Believe in You"

Another problem with giving aid too freely when working with the materially poor is it subconsciously tells them they are incapable. We give needy people things when they seem incapable of getting it on their own. Consequently, when you give a poor man something, you remind him you do not believe in his ability to provide for himself. Of course, this is not your goal, but it tends to be the byproduct of ongoing aid. It becomes a continual reminder that you deem them incapable of helping themselves.

James Shikwati was born in Kenya in 1970. Raised without many of the comforts we enjoy in developed countries, he knows what it is to live in grinding poverty while witnessing the ravages of famine and disease. But as a young schoolteacher in Kenya, Shikwati witnessed something else as well. He observed firsthand the effect of misguided aid. He watched as foreign governments dumped subsidized agricultural products into their markets, making it nearly impossible for local farmers to compete. How will a farmer sell his crop when an organization is handing out the product down the street? He observed farmers just giving up, not planting crops for fear of no market. In one interview with a newspaper, he pleaded with Western governments, "Please, stop this aid!"[2]

This plea from an African man caught the world's attention. Some immediately tried to use his comments as proof that aid to impoverished countries does more harm than good. Why not just focus more of our resources on ourselves since the aid we send over there isn't helping anyway? Others, primarily governments and organizations who had been sending the aid, denounced Shikwati's comments, calling them "misguided and shockingly wrong."

So who is right? Should we just keep our resources here? After all, even in wealthy countries roads always need repair, buildings could be nicer, and a myriad of proposed improvements could make our lives easier. Should we keep our surplus and continue making things better here?

Smart Aid

The answer is not to discontinue helping the poor. But we do need to reconsider how help is administered. Aid that leaves people in ongoing poverty less capable of taking care of their own needs should be redirected. Instead of introducing an agricultural product that undercuts and destroys the local farmer, why not use funds instead to buy these products from the local farmers and encourage local

> *The same dollar that can create and encourage paternalism can also encourage sustainable change. Aid is not the culprit; poor methods are.*

production? This practice, increasingly implemented in many aid organizations, not only helps the hungry but also encourages local industry. In short, what we need is not less aid but smart aid—aid that addresses the underlying problems.

The same dollar that can create and encourage paternalism can also encourage sustainable change. Aid is not the culprit; poor methods are. There is a time to freely give, and we will look at this more later. But we need to be aware of our tendency, both at home and abroad, to create paternalism. Steve Corbett and Brian Fikkert, in their book *When Helping Hurts*, give this important advice: "Do not do things for people that they can do for themselves. Memorize this, recite it under your breath all day long, and wear it like a garland around your neck. Every time you are engaged in poverty-alleviation ministry, keep this in the forefront of your mind, for it can keep you from doing all sorts of harm."[3]

Conclusion

One of the most challenging aspects of working with the poor is the reality that I am shaping their thinking regarding themselves. The simple fact that you come from America is enough to convince many people in these impoverished nations that you have all knowledge. After all, aren't you the one who just arrived in their village driving a vehicle worth more money than they will see in a lifetime? Didn't you just fly on a shiny jetliner? Surely you must have all the right answers and a proper understanding of how to do things.

So be very careful what you think about the poor, because your opinion of their abilities will over time become their opinion of themselves. If you think they are hopeless and helpless, then you will probably head down the paternalistic road, and before long they will begin to think of themselves as hopeless and helpless as well. But if you can see them as fellow children of God with abilities and local resources that they can utilize to provide for themselves, they will begin to think of themselves the same way. And as they begin to focus on and develop the resources God has placed in their care, real change can begin to occur.

Needing the Needy

Afew years ago I was visiting a secular microfinance organization in a deeply impoverished country. The branch manager, obviously pleased with the success of their loan program, told how it had started and the spectacular growth it had experienced. The program began with small loans to help impoverished individuals start businesses and provide for their families. It was a good model, and they had seen many families improve their material lives. But the longer I listened, the more disappointed I became. They had originally started their program with a clear mission and business model to achieve their goals. But it seemed that along the way they somehow lost their initial vision.

Their clients were required to pay interest on their loans, and this interest income seemed to have become the focus. As the loan manager explained their program, it didn't take long to calculate the tremendous income being produced by their huge loan portfolio! No longer were clients encouraged to get out of debt or graduate from the program. Instead, the manager told me, they try to keep their long-term clients since they pose little risk and bring in the greatest return. Those clients' successful stories would inspire generous donors and bring in even more donations.

This mindset also changed their day-to-day operations on the ground. No longer did they focus on teaching good business practices or even health and hygiene. Teaching programs are expensive to run, and their focus had shifted to portfolio growth and return on investment. And perhaps the most chilling reality was that they needed these needy people to make it all work! Why teach people to live sustainable lives if it will destroy your business model?

Needing the Needy

While preparing for this book, I had the opportunity to talk to many people involved in helping the poor. Some of these people work with situations where solutions are hard to find. Many do an admirable job, pouring their lives into blessing and helping those in great spiritual and physical need. But one comment that stuck with me came from a man who manages several large aid programs. We talked about some of the challenges he faces, about new methods used today, and the impact on his work if the people he is currently helping would be taught sustainability and suddenly didn't need him.

"But if that would happen," he said with concern, "what would happen to our programs? And what about our donors? What would we do about them?"

I left this discussion with a strange mixture of emotions. Wasn't the original goal to help needy people help themselves? Why should the thought of meeting objectives concern him? The answer to this question is sobering and should be considered by all of us. Our vision, both as individuals and as organizations, can subtly shift over time.

From Results to Revenue

Most charitable organizations initially form because of a desire to address a need. Aware of a particular problem, they long to bring assistance, and their focus is only on fixing the problem. They want to bring relief as quickly and efficiently as possible. They want results.

To meet this objective, they tell others. If they have a worthy cause and a generous donor base, funds will begin to flow toward the need. But as the organizational machine is built, the original objective can gradually be forgotten.

Instead of focusing on results, it is possible to begin focusing on the need for revenue. Funds can become the focus, and less and less thought is given to whether or not they affect the change the organization originally wanted. When visits are made to the field, the goal can shift to getting stories and pictures to increase revenue, rather than ascertaining that the aid is actually producing results. As I listened to this aid manager, that was what I heard. They needed the needy to keep revenue flowing to their organization.

A Personal Need for the Needy

This principle, however, doesn't apply only to organizations. This danger of needing the needy affects each of us individually as well.

We like to feel appreciated. We want to see results from our daily activities. We need the affirmation that comes from blessing others, and we like to fix things or people. I believe God gives us this trait. And this need for affirmation coupled with our desire to be fixers brings us to an obvious conclusion: we need people or things to fix in order to feel affirmed. We need the needy so that we can feel fulfilled.

Counselors refer to this condition, when out of control, as codependency. Codependent people constantly try to assist those with needs. They can't stand the thought of being alone and unneeded. But it is important to understand that codependency does not refer to *all* feelings of concern for others. It refers to people who do this in an unhealthy manner or to an excessive degree. The motivation can be more about me and my needs than the person or situation I am supposedly trying to help.

But this condition is not confined to the realm of counseling. We find the same problem in helping people deal with material poverty. In our eagerness, for whatever reason, to bestow gifts on someone, we become more focused on our need to give than on the recipient's need to receive. And it doesn't always happen off in some foreign country. It can happen in our local congregations, in our communities, and even in governments.

Following the rapid westward expansion in America during the early 1800s, the general public felt a great deal of guilt toward Native Americans, and rightfully so. The settlers and their government made and broke treaty after treaty, grabbing up land and abusing the American Indians they had stolen the land from. As a result, the government has often attempted to placate the Indians and ease the pain of guilt.

Several years ago I helped in a building project on an Indian reservation. As part of the contract, we were required to hire a certain percentage of workers from the local Native American population. But even as we prepared the bid for this project, we expected these workers would be a liability. They have received monthly government checks for so long that their work ethic has been destroyed. Trash surrounds many houses, their front yards are filled with tall weeds growing up through old cars, and theft is a major problem. It is sad to see these extremely resourceful people, who for many generations had survived the harsh conditions on the prairie, almost totally destroyed by indiscriminate aid. But America still deals with guilt from the past, and continuing to send those monthly checks provides some relief from that pain.

This need to give for our own good can produce disturbing results in our communities and churches as well. Recently I heard of an alcoholic father who, feeling great remorse for the effect his habit had on his family, decided to give his son a large monthly allowance. This made the father feel better, but it destroyed the son. The son could see through this hypocrisy and rebelled against both the authority of his father and local church. The father found relief from his guilt but ignored the long-term effect on his son. He was giving, but his giving was driven by a selfish motive.

Again, the point here is not that we should stop giving; rather, it is that we keep our focus on the real needs of the individuals we are trying to help. Continuing to give money to that brother in your congregation who habitually struggles with poor management may feel good. It may give you a sense of fulfillment and help assuage the guilt resulting from your own affluent lifestyle. But is it actually helping him? Is continually helping him avoid the consequences of poor choices and lack of planning going to bless his family? No, we learn by facing the consequences of our choices. If this brother is like most in this condition, he probably needs improved management skills more than monetary gifts. Continuing to give may keep him from confronting and addressing his actual lack. But let's look at another reason we need the needy.

Our God-Plex
Most humans sense they need a god to save them. Those of us who believe in the Almighty God of the Bible understand this and see our Lord Jesus as the only Saviour of the world. But many unbelievers,

when in difficulty, call on some kind of perceived deity to help them out of their crises. They may believe that one god got them into trouble, but they typically will call on another to get them out. This trait of saving people is an attribute of God that we like to imitate. We like to be saviors too.

As a small lad, I played out in the dirt behind the house with my toy trucks and tractor. To someone looking on, I was just a dirty little boy at play. But in my mind there was much more going on. I couldn't tell you how many entire villages I saved back there behind the house. I would concoct all manner of scenarios where the town was just about to be annihilated by a flood or an approaching enemy. Time after time my quick thinking and calmness in the face of approaching catastrophe saved the day.

Somehow I never tired of developing and playing out these scenarios. I wanted to be a savior like God.

But this same tendency, which appears foolish and even humorous in a child, can have sinister results when trying to help the hurting. When I become more interested in fulfilling my desire to "save" people than actually searching for their long-term blessing, it can produce lasting harm.

Looking back, I know I have harmed people by this twisted mentality. It has caused me to ignore facts and create mental arguments explaining why my aid helps. It has diminished my desire to investigate, for fear that I might find my aid wasn't really helping. This would destroy my opportunity to "save." Relief experts have coined the phrase "god-plex" to describe this human tendency. Sadly, this is all too common and has greatly deterred real, sustainable change in many situations.

Conclusion

It is possible, even with the best intentions, to gradually shift our focus from the needs of others to our own. But this doesn't have to occur. In fact, for most of my life I have been surrounded by believers who willingly sacrifice their own desires for the good of others. I have had the opportunity to work with many people who demonstrate the character of Jesus as they reach out to the poor.

Notice how the Apostle Paul describes the example Jesus left us. Paul gave the church at Corinth an abundance of good exhortation about helping the hurting church at Jerusalem, much of it regarding the mechanics of giving and the need for accountability. But Paul backed up and pointed at the Lord Jesus as an example of pure motives. He said, "For ye know the grace of our Lord Jesus Christ, that, though he was rich, yet for your sakes he became poor, that ye through his poverty might be rich."[a] Notice Paul's words, "for your sakes." Jesus' motive in abandoning Himself to save mankind wasn't to make Him feel better. Instead, He focused on our need. Jesus gave Himself for our sakes. And as His followers, may we also focus our efforts on the needs of others.

---

[a] 2 Corinthians 8:9

Short-Term Missions—
Avoiding the Pitfalls

I t was the morning of November 16, 2010, when Juan Andres drove his car to the U.S.-Mexico border and prepared to cross. He had only a three-and-a-half-mile commute each day from his home in Mexico to his job at the University of Texas in El Paso. To expedite this daily commute, Juan had applied for and received a special pass from the U.S. Customs department. This enabled him to cross without the normal vehicle check others were required to comply with.

But on this morning, officials singled him out for a random check and discovered two bags of marijuana hidden in his trunk. Although Juan insisted he was innocent, there was no evidence that the trunk had been tampered with, and he was arrested and placed in custody. Juan had no idea how those two black duffle bags had found their way into his trunk, and he was scared.

"I was afraid of what could happen to my family. I was trying to figure out who could have done that, and nothing came to my imagination. We really didn't have enemies or know people who were involved in that," he said, referring to the marijuana.[1]

Nevertheless, Juan was charged with drug possession with the intent to distribute, and he spent the next six months in jail awaiting trial. He could have taken what is known as a "safety valve" plea, which is an option for first-time drug-trafficking offenders with little or no criminal history, but he didn't. Juan knew he was innocent, and he hoped the jury would be able to see the truth. But they didn't.

On May 10, Juan was pronounced guilty and faced up to three years in prison. But three days after his trial, Juan was suddenly called back into court for a status hearing and released the same day. This dramatic change of events occurred because U.S. District Judge David

Briones suddenly became aware of a pattern. He noticed that several other cases had been almost identical to Juan's. In each case, two black duffle bags containing marijuana were transported by an unsuspecting driver with a special pass from the U.S. Customs department. The FBI investigated the cases and exposed an undercover plan by a drug cartel that, aware of the special pass given to certain commuters, had concocted a plan to take advantage of it.

Scouts hired by the cartel monitored these commuters, especially those with consistent routines, noting the time of day they passed and the makes and models of their cars. After identifying potential targets, the scouts followed them on the Mexican side of the border, copied their vehicle identification numbers, and then used them to have keys made by a locksmith. Once they had keys on each side of the border, they could simply put bags of marijuana in the trunks on the Mexican side and retrieve them while the car was parked along the street in the United States. The American government report referred to the unsuspecting drug transporters as "blind mules."

As I read this account, I couldn't help but think of our many attempts at cross-cultural mission work. It's not unusual to see short-term mission teams while standing in security lines in foreign airports. You can almost always identify these teams by matching, brightly colored tee-shirts, bright smiles, and excited voices. When I have opportunity, I enjoy talking to these people as they return home. They are usually full of stories and are eager to tell about their encounters with "the natives." They left home with a desire to bless, and they return home convinced they made a difference.

But sometimes these teams remind me of the "blind mules" inadvertently carrying marijuana in from Mexico. I say inadvertently, because these teams have no desire to harm anyone. Yet I am convinced it is extremely difficult to cross cultural lines without doing some damage. Most of these volunteers come with the latest in cameras, iPods, and other gadgetry unknown in the local culture. They view a daily change of clothes, especially in hot climates, as simply proper hygiene, while the locals may view it as an impossible luxury. When volunteers arrive in a Toyota Land Cruiser, they may be driving something of more value than several of the local families' combined income for a lifetime. Like "blind mules," we may unknowingly carry things into a foreign setting that are a detriment to their community and Christian lives. We need to understand that in our attempt to impact their lives for good, we might achieve the opposite. We can leave behind a discontentment that didn't exist before we arrived. This is the reality of cross-cultural missions.

My goal is not to discourage us from helping those in need. We who live in developed countries should be doing more, not less. My burden is that we understand the potential we have to unintentionally damage, and then take steps and use methods that continue to bless those in need long after we have gone home. The sooner we become aware of the long-term problems our short-term solutions leave behind, the better. Let's look at some things we need to consider before heading off.

The Need for Humility

In 1800, only 1 percent of Protestant Christians lived outside North America and Western Europe. By 1900, the number had grown to 10 percent, and by 2000 it had

> *The sooner we become aware of the long-term problems our short-term solutions leave behind, the better.*

increased to more than 65 percent. Christianity's center of gravity shifted. Today, the largest concentration of professing Protestant Christians is not in the United States, but in Africa and Latin America.[2]

But though this shift has occurred, sometimes we act as if we are still the center of the world. We could learn so much from believers in other parts of the world if we would only humble ourselves enough to listen. This unwillingness to listen is noticed. Many Christian leaders comment on the lack of questions from visiting American pastors. We go to tell others how we do things in the States and use our churches as an example of what theirs should look like. But our efforts would be more effective if we could learn from their persistence in prayer, their patience in dealing with major obstacles, and the way they assist each other in difficulty. Now make no mistake. There is a tremendous need for instruction in many of these countries. But as we go to help, let's go humbly, acknowledging we have much to learn as well.

Part of our problem stems from our own culture. Americans are known around the world for being ignorant of other cultures and insensitive toward them. I heard recently that Ethiopian Airlines regularly receives phone calls from Americans who ask if they need to bring their own food for overseas flights. In an American's mind, Ethiopia means poverty and starvation, and we can't envision a good meal on one of their flights. We tend to assume everything is wonderful here, that there is no place like the good old USA, and life is awful everywhere else.

But although much of the world does experience deep poverty, North America is not the only nice place to live. The world is big, and many other countries have a good economy and material prosperity as well. I remember a discussion with a young woman in Honduras years ago. There is much poverty in Honduras, but this young lady always had her needs supplied. As we talked about her experience living there, I realized she had no real interest in even visiting the United States, and she definitely didn't want to live there. I was shocked! In my egocentric mindset I had assumed everyone wanted what we have and longed to move here. This young woman was educated, and the arrogant attitudes she had observed in visiting Americans had not impressed her. We need to remember that others appreciate their cultures and countries and have much to contribute to the church of Christ.

Recently I received a letter from a brother who spent several years living among the people in a very poor developing country. He had farmed with them as he tried to reach out with the Gospel, and over time they came to accept him as one of their own. In his letter he said this:

> I remember an American team coming up our little river to hold evangelistic crusades. They used the schoolhouse right across the river from our house, so we paddled over to hear them, and the evening stands out in my memory as an example of all the wrong ways of doing things. The American speakers that night made it clear to us that we were very fortunate to have them leave the comforts of the United States

and their large churches to come speak to ignorant backwater hicks like us.

They provided a weak salvation sermon and got one or two responses from people whom I knew personally, and who never displayed a hint of fruit after their supposed conversion. But of course the team videotaped the whole service, and footage of those people was presumably displayed back in the States to back up the claims of many conversions. The icing on the cake was when they handed out candy to adults and children alike after the service, again videotaping the "poor natives" gratefully receiving a handout.

I looked into the eyes of my neighbors, the people who worked just as hard as I did for just as little money, and we all understood each other. These Americans didn't have a clue. They would die of starvation if they were dropped off on one of our farms with only a machete and a shovel. They couldn't paddle a boat to save their lives, and they understood nothing of our world.

Furthermore, I suspected this trip was not really to help us, but rather to boost their credentials back home as magnanimous and mission-minded saints. Without speaking a word, we all agreed to just humor them and pretend we appreciated their condescending version of help.

Perhaps the writer of this letter was wrong and misguided in his assessment, but I don't think so. Far too many stories out there carry a similar message, and it is time to recognize our great need for humility as we reach out to others.

The Need for Patience
I like to structure the time in my day, make lists, and check tasks off as I complete them. A day, in my mind, is an allotment of time wherein as many tasks as possible are to be completed. Therefore I run into trouble when entering most impoverished countries where the people are less time-oriented and more relationship-oriented. I remember some

of the first short-term missions I was involved in. I was ready to hit the ground running and get the project finished. I had, and still struggle with, a checklist mentality. It was as though I believed these people were not capable of constructing a building, and erecting it swiftly was my primary goal. But there is something we need to remember. Those of us who have grown up in a time-oriented culture have the potential of creating much long-term damage in a short amount of time in countries that value relationships.

I recently read about a team that traveled to Honduras. They went to build two houses in a poor neighborhood, and at the conclusion they went home feeling good about what they had done. Two new houses were built, an obvious testimony to the team's self-

> *Those of us who have grown up in a time-oriented culture have the potential of creating much long-term damage in a short amount of time.*

sacrifice and hard work. After they went home, someone asked a local bricklayer about the project and how he felt about it. This man had been asked to help with the construction and had been excited at first. But his initial enthusiasm didn't last long. "I found out soon enough that I was in the way," he said. "The group wanted to do things their way and made me feel like I didn't know what I was doing. I helped only the first day."[3]

That work team went home totally unaware of the feelings they left behind. But with just a little patience and willingness to listen, the story could have turned out totally different. They could have encouraged this local bricklayer and even taught him better techniques. Instead, they left him feeling inferior and of little value. Not only that, they probably missed a chance to learn some things from him. People who have grown up in poverty are by necessity often very resourceful. I remember watching in amazement as a man in one of those countries joined two pieces of PVC pipe together without any pipe fittings. I didn't know this was even possible! If we can keep our eyes open and be patient, there is much we can learn.

The Need for Discernment in Giving

Those who serve in a developing country for any length of time usually come to appreciate the importance of indigenous sustainability. After some bumps and bruises, they see the great need to work slowly with the locals, teaching them the blessing of saving and using the resources they have. But it takes only a short time for a newcomer to destroy this developing mindset. Several years ago in West Africa, a missionary medical doctor was trying to teach a local congregation how to work toward the goal of locally funded church planting. After two years, the doctor was elated when the pastor reported that the congregation had increased their savings for outreach from forty-five dollars the year before to sixty-one dollars this year. It was truly a time for rejoicing. The congregation felt they had achieved something together and began working toward planting a new church several kilometers away.

But during this time a short-term missionary came and spent some time with the congregation. She didn't see a group of people learning the blessing of working together toward a common goal. All she saw was their poverty from her perspective. Consequently, she gave them a gift—$6,800 to help their efforts.[4] Now imagine the impact that sum of money had on this congregation. It resulted in the pastor abandoning the initial savings project and throwing his efforts into looking for other wealthy foreigners who would be willing to give. The original vision was scuttled, and one can feel only compassion for the medical doctor. He saw all he had been trying to teach the locals for the past two years go down the drain. Unfortunately, many short-termers have no idea of the impact of giving too much too fast.

The Need to Analyze Motives

Earlier we discussed the importance of honestly analyzing our motives in giving. This is especially true when considering short-term missions. No doubt, a certain glamour accompanies projects away from home, and especially overseas. Are we really attempting to help the people there, or is the primary goal to change ourselves and our youth? I believe short-term missions can bless those who go. But let's be honest about what we are doing. In our eagerness to expand the minds of our youth, it is important to not forget the potential we have to harm the ones we go to serve.

It is also important to not elevate one type of service above another. Be careful about coming home and telling others how much was accomplished. There may be people in your congregation who actually accomplished more than you did, quietly visiting rest homes and working with those who are struggling while you were gone. Make sure their efforts are acknowledged as well.

The Need to Keep Helping

In this chapter I have laid out many downsides to short-term missions. But my goal has not been to discourage you from going. There is great need in many parts of the globe, and we who live in developed countries have a great responsibility. I have seen pastors in China who will risk their lives just to receive a few hours of doctrinal teaching. There are people in areas of deep poverty who would walk miles to receive basic business teaching from an American businessman. There are many medical clinics around the globe being run by medical staff with only a few weeks of formal training. They would love to have a doctor or nurse spend a week with them, teaching new techniques and better procedures. Needs abound, and we have much to offer. But we also have much to learn. So as we go, let's listen and learn. The body of Christ isn't confined to one continent, and we have no right to say, "I have no need of you. Nay, much more those members of the body, which seem to be more feeble, are necessary."[a]

Conclusion

In modern Christianity it is popular to "go on a mission," and there are times when this can bless both those who go and those who receive help. The early church also sent people out when there was a need. But it is entirely possible for short-term missions to distract us from God's best. God still intends for each congregation to be a mission station, and your mission isn't over when you return from a mission trip. Viewing your local congregation as a mission station should impact every part of your life. It will affect how you use "your" time, talents, and

[a] 1 Corinthians 12:21, 22

money, not just when you are "on a mission," but in everyday life. It will affect how you view your neighbors, business associates, and even your competitors.

It will also change how you view yourself and what you expect to get out of your endeavor when you serve away from home. It is possible, in these endeavors, to subconsciously focus on what the trip or project will do for me, thus becoming another example of needing the needy.

But perhaps this is another area where we can learn from our brothers and sisters in other parts of the world. Remember, some of them send out missionaries as well. But sometimes their expectations can sound quite different. While many Americans go expecting upscale hotels, a great chance to see the world, and wonderful shopping opportunities, listen to what Chinese missionaries expect when they go. In his book, *Back to Jerusalem,* Brother Yun says, "Thousands of young men and women in China will go as missionaries who are not afraid to die for Jesus . . . they are not only willing to die for the Gospel, they are expecting it."[5] Let their example challenge you.

Unintended Consequences at Home

The late 1800s were a time of radical transformation in America. Almost every cultural norm was challenged. In school we learned that it was called the Industrial Revolution, and that this cultural upheaval rapidly changed the daily lives of millions of people. Transportation, communication, agriculture, medicine—things that had experienced little change for centuries—were suddenly transformed forever. Life for most would never be the same.

But as we now know, not all of this change was good. The family structure weakened as fathers left home to begin working in factories so that they could afford wonderful new inventions their society now offered. Suddenly there were more options, contentment seemed more elusive, consumer debt was introduced, and people carried around a longer wish list.

But this era changed more than just society and business; it changed churches as well. After experiencing years of persecution and turmoil in Europe, many Christians immigrated to America, searching for a place to live out their faith in peace. Some came with evangelistic fire, but many came looking for safety and tranquility. At first there were forests to clear, roads to construct, and businesses to build. But following the initial labor of settling a new country and dealing with the impact of the Revolutionary War, a time of peace and plenty followed. For several generations, many lived quiet lives, raising large families in nice rural settings and seldom leaving their local communities. Religious life became peaceful and predictable.

But during the late 1800s, following the Civil War, the winds of change began to blow. Cities expanded, and life picked up speed. Better communication quickly brought new ideas into communities and homes.

New modes of transportation moved and mixed a better educated populace, and suddenly change seemed exciting and good. New ideas and ways of doing things popped up everywhere, and new methods began showing up in churches as well. The list of changes introduced during this period of time is dizzying. The 1800s saw the influx of Sunday Schools, camp meetings, altar calls, and mission boards. For the first time, many conservative churches were being told of the importance of having educated leaders.

Change seemed to be everywhere. As one Anabaptist writer said, "Suddenly, in the 1870s young Mennonite preachers appeared from 'out west'—out in Illinois where they had attended D.L. Moody's Bible school. Like a forest fire their new style of preaching swept the congregations of eastern Pennsylvania. Revival meetings lasted week after week. At altar calls in packed churches, some who responded had to step to the front on backs of benches after aisles got full. Everyone, it seemed, was gloriously 'getting saved.' Then Sunday schools, mission conferences, and young people's Bible schools drove the need to 'spread the good news of salvation' deep into the hearts of 'awakened' souls."[1]

It seemed exciting things were happening everywhere! And it all seemed so wonderful, as churches during this time experienced phenomenal expansion. Carl Bowman, in his book *Brethren Society,*[2] records that the Brethren church grew from about 11,000 members in 1850 to approximately 77,000 by 1900.

And then there were the exciting mission stories. New methods of communication and travel, coupled with literature describing the reality of spiritual and material poverty around the globe, brought the world's needs right into many homes. Families sat entranced listening to stories from remote places around the world where the need was great. And they responded! Many opened their hearts and wallets to assist in this great cause. Men headed off to foreign countries, some knowing they might never return. It was an exciting time to be alive, and for many it must have seemed revival had come. But looking back on history from our vantage point, the picture isn't quite as clear.

Many of those churches, within a very short time, could hardly be called conservative. Many discarded valuable doctrines along the way, compromising Biblical principles and gradually blending into mainstream America. In short, things didn't turn out like many of these churches anticipated. They went out optimistically to change the world through mission work, but in many cases the world changed them. While focusing on reaching out to others, they lost their balance and their grip on holiness. How did this happen? Why did so many churches during this time lose their separation from the world, nonresistant principles, and many of the clear teachings in Scripture? What caused the compromise and doctrinal washout during those years?

This is not a question to lightly brush over. Humans are famous for not learning from history, and followers of Christ have proved no exception. If we can learn from looking back, we want to do this and hopefully avoid those same pitfalls. But even more important to our focus in this book, did missions and certain methods of reaching over the wall to the needy cause this radical change?

> *Humans are famous for not learning from history.*

Are there lessons we can gain from those in the past who have tried to share spiritually and materially with those in need? How do we avoid these negative unintended consequences?

I believe there are lessons we can learn, but it is important to carefully analyze the cause. When we diagnose the root cause of a problem, we also unwittingly select a cure. Those nurses in Panama decided pans of water were the solution simply because they had mistakenly identified ants as the root cause of malaria. Because they misdiagnosed the root cause, the problem not only continued, but was compounded. Those pans of water produced unintended consequences they could not have imagined, simply because they misdiagnosed the root cause. So let's carefully look at some potential causes to the spiritual decline and doctrinal washout that occurred.

Foreign Missions?

Some have concluded that the rapid spiritual decline that began in the late 1800s was due to the focus on missions. Missionaries sent out from many quiet, conservative congregations experienced excitement and revival on the mission field such as they had never known. After seeing the Spirit move in a mighty way in foreign lands, all the strict modes and methods, details of clothing, and warnings from elderly ministers seemed insignificant. Why focus on all these unimportant details when such exciting things were happening?

Little by little, changes were made, and before long churches drifted far from their original position on many important doctrinal issues. The missionaries coming back had a powerful influence on many churches. And if you decide a focus on outreach is the root cause of spiritual decline, the solution is obvious—don't have organized missions.

Separation From the World?

Others have said that since Jesus, the early church, and the early Anabaptists emphasized outreach, sending people out could not be the root cause of spiritual decline. Rather, the decline started when the church began to shift their focus away from staying separate from the world. If the believers had reminded themselves of who they were, things would have turned out much differently.

If you conclude the root cause of spiritual decline is a lack of separation from the world, then the obvious answer is to focus on separation. Many congregations did this. They began to focus on their church standards, holding tighter to them in an attempt to avoid worldliness and spiritual compromise. Even as they went to foreign lands with the Gospel, they insisted that the converts comply with these standards even though they were not relevant there. Now they had missions as well as separation from the world. But difficulties develop when standards are implemented that new believers from another culture cannot identify with. Every society has its own set of challenges. And trying to impose solutions from one culture onto another has the potential to confuse the very people we want to enlighten.

Appreciation for Heritage?

Still others have said the problem was a general lack of appreciation for spiritual heritage. Believers forgot where they came from and how valiantly their forefathers had fought for the basic Scriptural principles they were laying aside. And if forgetting our heritage is the root problem of doctrinal washout, the answer is increased teaching on church history. We should teach our children why our denomination is different from another and why it is important to maintain what has been given to us. All of us can think of churches that have focused almost exclusively on preserving a certain way of life.

But when this becomes our primary focus, the result is individuals who are much better versed in their way of life than in the Gospel of Jesus Christ. This approach is likely to produce people who go through the outward motions of a separated life, yet show little evidence of being born again.

The Root Cause
The list of potential root causes for the obvious spiritual decline since the mid 1800s would be a long one. Many books have been written, messages preached, and ideas proposed to explain this downward spiral. Perhaps it is presumptuous to assume we could explain exactly what happened during this time period, or even shine new light on it. I believe all the arguments and explanations above have some validity. It is true that missionaries impacted their local congregations upon returning home, and this brought consequences. It is also true that many did not put enough emphasis on separation from the world and did not properly appreciate their heritage.

But while each of these observations has some validity, I want you to consider that perhaps none of these are actually the root cause.

Remember, in the mid-1800s the spiritual climate in many churches appeared dry to zealous youth. Life seemed monotonous to many, and as the exciting fire of Protestant revivalism and change began to sweep over America, it seemed like the rest of Christianity was alive and they were dead. Conservative youth compared the excitement happening in other churches to their own dull customs, and dissatisfaction set in. These zealous youth probably felt a little ashamed of their local churches. Why should they continue to go through the same boring routine each

Sunday when new and better ways produced such exciting results?

Becoming dissatisfied with the status quo is not inherently wrong. The search for something better has led to many great personal and collective revivals. No, the problem wasn't necessarily that these young men became dissatisfied. I would suggest the problem lay in where they turned for answers.

Who Are We Following?

Rather than going back to the Bible and the historical example of the Anabaptist revival, which call believers to live out the teachings of Jesus Christ, these men began to imitate the methods and theology of their Protestant neighbors. Instead of emphasizing a changed life by following

> *Modern Christianity has shifted from focusing on a change in life to a change in belief.*

Jesus, the focus shifted to what a person knows and believes *about* Him.

This subtle change may not seem important, but the consequences were dramatic and had huge ramifications. Suddenly, living out the teachings of Jesus did not seem nearly as important as how much Bible knowledge you had attained. The earliest believers were known as disciples, or followers of Jesus, and indeed they did follow. In the book of Acts we find that they later received another name—Christians.[a]

A shift occurred, and if you check a Merriam-Webster dictionary today, the definition for *Christian* says nothing about imitating the life of Jesus. Rather, a Christian is "one who professes belief in the teachings of Jesus Christ." Modern Christianity has shifted from focusing on a change in life to a change in belief. This change of focus is huge, and I believe it is the underlying root cause of the doctrinal slide of the late 1800s.

But this shift didn't only affect our history. It still affects us today. It continues to plague our churches and our outreach, and even the secular world is aware of this dramatic change. A few years ago an author interviewed in a secular news magazine stated that the weakening of

---

[a] Acts 11:26

Christianity has come from within "the churches themselves, when they started focusing on loving Jesus, rather than listening to Him."[3] Jesus plainly said that those who love Him will keep His commandments, yet as this author points out, Christianity has so diluted the Gospel that verbal adoration is replacing simple obedience to what He says.

> *But if we make either outreach or separation from the world our primary target, we will steer off course. We are called to follow Jesus and to apply His teachings to our lives.*

Anyone who follows and imitates the life of Christ will live separate from the world and will appreciate a godly heritage. He will have a burden for souls and a strong desire to reach the lost. But if we make either outreach or separation from the world our primary target, we will steer off course. We are called to follow Jesus and to apply His teachings to our lives, or perhaps we should say, apply our lives to His teachings. When we begin focusing primarily on some other target, regardless how noble, we will find ourselves somewhere God never intended.

Following Jesus

Do the teachings of Jesus scare you? Do you find yourself avoiding some of His teachings because they make you uneasy and conflict with your lifestyle? Søren Kierkegaard was a Danish Lutheran writer during the nineteenth century who became critical of the church in Denmark. He wrote some scathing comments as he observed the lives of professing believers in his time, but perhaps we can learn from his words.

> The matter is quite simple. The Bible is very easy to understand. But we Christians are a bunch of scheming swindlers. We pretend to be unable to understand it because we know very well that the minute we understand, we are obliged to act accordingly. Take any words in the New Testament and forget everything except pledging yourself to act accordingly. You will say, If I do that my whole life will be ruined. How would I ever get on in the world? Herein lies the real place of Christian

scholarship. Christian scholarship is the Church's prodigious invention to defend itself against the Bible, to ensure that we can continue to be good Christians without the Bible coming too close. Oh, priceless scholarship, what would we do without you? Dreadful it is to fall into the hands of the living God. Yes it is even dreadful to be alone with the New Testament.[4]

This quote contains a powerful thought and a challenge. Our seminars, books, sermons, and even denominational standards, as good as they may be, can be used to defend ourselves against the teachings of Jesus. If I focus on how much better I am keeping my church's standards than others, for example, then I can defend myself against those teachings of Jesus regarding wealth that threaten to turn my life upside down. Or if I focus on the errors of those who have failed in their mission attempts, I can defend myself against the call of Jesus to love and reach out to my neighbors, wherever they live, Bible study, analysis of history, theology, or a focus on legalism in the church can all distract from following the teachings of Jesus. None of these things are wrong in themselves until they compete with following Him.

How many church divisions, family conflicts, or failed mission attempts go back to focusing on something other than Jesus? How often do we become caught up in good things but fail to focus on following Him? How much time do you spend reading the teachings of Jesus and then going out and attempting to live them out in His strength? As Jesus Himself asked, "Why call ye me, Lord, Lord, and do not the things which I say?"[b]

Conclusion

Historically, the country of Rwanda had been regarded as one of the most Christian countries in Africa. The Roman Catholics began working there in 1900, the Lutherans in 1907, and later they were followed by Baptists, Anglicans, and other Protestant missionaries. Many indigenous churches sprang up, and by 1946 an estimated 90 percent of the tribal leaders were professing Christians, and the king officially declared Rwanda a Christian nation.

---

[b] Luke 6:46

But underneath all this change in outward belief there remained tribal and ethnic tension. Even though the picture looked devout on the surface, feelings from the past lingered. Missionaries talked about the great success in converting the country and used the strong churches in Rwanda as an example for other countries. But in April 1994, the country erupted in civil war. The savage carnage that followed defies description. Within just a few days, almost a million Rwandans were slaughtered, and millions more were displaced, fleeing for their lives. Many Rwandans will never forget the terrible sight of thousands of corpses floating silently down the river Akagera and on to Lake Victoria. But they weren't the only ones in shock.

> *There is a great difference between changing a man's stated belief and changing the man.*

Many missionaries who had lived among these people were left in shock as well. What went wrong? How could a supposedly converted people suddenly act like wild savages, many even slaughtering neighbors within their own church fellowship? One missionary wrote, "On Sundays in Rwanda we used to see well-dressed neighbors walking to church on every road. Yet, last year these same neighbors slaughtered each other."[5] How could this happen?

There is a great difference between changing a man's stated belief and changing the man.

Conversion is more than just raising your hand, reciting a prayer, or going forward after an emotionally charged revival meeting. It is more than just joining a church or being baptized. It begins with true repentance and belief in Jesus. It is an obedient, love-faith relationship with Jesus Christ that is always following and imitating His life. It is daily, by His strength, becoming more and more conformed to the image of Christ in our daily walk. Anything less will produce unintended consequences.

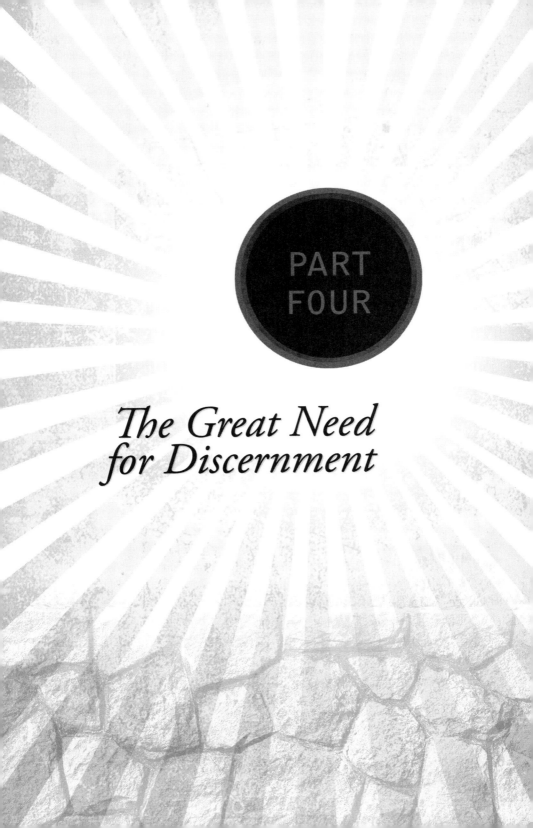

PART
FOUR

*The Great Need
for Discernment*

Money, Management, or Mentoring?

H ow could so many disruptive things happen to one man in such a short time? It seemed every part of Jim's life was under attack, and it all came crashing down on him within just a few months. He had been carrying a high level of consumer debt before the crisis hit, so when he lost his job, Jim was forced to find less expensive housing. He had just settled into his smaller home when his child was injured in an accident. This not only meant Jim faced large medical bills, but it also kept him away from his new job for several months. The combination of accumulated consumer debt, lower income, and large medical bills shook Jim to the core. During those few months he must have felt like a modern-day Job.

But Jim wasn't alone. Jim belonged to a vibrant church fellowship, and as they saw all his trials, they responded beautifully. Meals were brought in, people stopped by to help, and Jim's family experienced the blessing of belonging to the body of Christ. Something else happened as well. Money began to pour into their mailbox. It seemed every day brought more checks, cash, and money orders. After people stopped by to visit, Jim's family often found cash lying somewhere in the house. Envelopes arrived, postmarked from distant states, stuffed with cash and having no return address. They were literally flooded with cash, more than enough to take care of the medical expenses and his time off work. Jim felt blessed and couldn't get done telling what a blessing this experience had been to his family. His extended church family, in return, encouraged Jim to let them know if more needs emerged in the future.

Time went on, and Jim's life eventually returned to normal—except for his financial life. His medical bills had all been paid and the string of problems that had plagued him went away, yet his consumer debt remained. Though Jim had received more than enough to repay his debts, the extra money had been spent on other things, and he found his debt load increasing. His credit cards were always at their limits, and he had trouble repaying loans from friends. But something was different now. Before he received all those gifts, Jim tried to reduce his spending whenever things got tight. Now he began to call on the individuals who had helped him before.

Jim had many good-hearted and well-meaning friends, and when he called and explained his situation, they responded by once again sending money. And, of course, each crisis was a real one. Life just kept sending problems he hadn't expected. His friends, still feeling sorry for poor Jim, had a difficult time saying no.

Years have passed, and to this day Jim still struggles financially. Various friends have become concerned and have tried to speak to Jim regarding his need for financial management. But as long as he can find people who feel sorry for "poor Jim," it will be difficult to convince him that his real need is management, not money.

Unfortunately, we all know of similar stories. We seem to be good at responding to an immediate crisis. Our hearts go out to those in difficulty, and this is commendable. Unfortunately, though, sometimes our efforts to help actually create long-term problems. How can we avoid this? How can we help the Jims out there without creating ongoing dependency? The answer to these questions lies in our ability to properly identify the actual need. Let's consider Jim's story. What could have been done differently?

Accountability in Christian Stewardship
One glaring deficiency in this story is financial accountability. Where were the leaders in this church? Why didn't Jim have brothers in his congregation who sat down with him, even before the major problems came, and addressed his consumer debt and financial issues? Weren't they aware of his poor management skills? Though we know how to provide accountability in some parts of our lives, when it comes to finances, we get a little squeamish. Recently a bishop told me that the members in his congregation are good at keeping an eye on each other,

except when it comes to the checkbook. Money is off limits unless there is a major problem.

But this is certainly different from the early church in the book of Acts. In chapters two and four, we find them opening up their finances, sharing, and holding each other accountable. While these accounts may have been given to share the Christian fiscal philosophy more than to prescribe a specific pattern, these earlier believers obviously were open with their personal finances. We should learn from their example. If there was ever a time when we need more discussion, more openness, and more accountability in our finances, it is now. Situations like Jim's occur because we don't see financial stewardship and careful accountability as important topics.

Need for Mentoring

Where were the spiritual and financial mentors in Jim's life? More important, who are they in your church? Do you have a plan for dealing with those who struggle? In the North American culture, time is usually deemed more valuable than money. Consequently, our first response to a need is most likely with money. Compounding this is the fact that, in most congregations, those who might have extra time are not always good managers. And those who have a gift in money management tend to be too busy to teach someone else. As a result, we tend to give money where management and mentoring are the real needs.

Mentoring is not easy and can be a thankless task. Informing someone that his lifestyle needs to change does not usually endear you to that person. But if we are serious about providing sustainable and beneficial help, we need good mentors who willingly sacrifice time and are backed by the congregation.

Let's go back to Jim's situation. When problems first poured into Jim's life, what was his need? In addition to his emotional needs, it was financial relief. He couldn't work, had medical bills, and didn't know where to turn. Of course, there should have been some accountability in how the money was given to him, but his primary need was money. But as time went on, the need changed. The emergency was over. No longer did he lack income, nor did he have medical bills he couldn't pay. His income stream was restored, and his real need changed from money to better management. Those he contacted for help didn't take time to investigate and therefore remained unaware of the change. They still felt sorry for "poor Jim."

Many of us don't take the time required to investigate problems. Consequently, our solutions sometimes intensify the problem and make it worse. Recently I was driving past an area in Haiti where tents and shacks had been constructed along the road after the earthquake. I couldn't help but feel compassion toward these people living along this busy, noisy road. But the person with me explained that few of these "homes" were actually occupied at night. The Haitians I saw really lived in the city but built these shacks along the road in hopes the sight would produce empathy (and cash) from those who pass. This scheme has been profitable for them, and each morning they travel from their homes in town to sit in front of their shack, hoping for handouts from missionaries, aid workers, and others who pass by.

But if these passersby would take time to investigate, they would find they are not actually helping those with the greatest need. Furthermore, giving to them only increases the number of beggars who believe wealthy foreigners are their best resource.

Conclusion

For many years, crosswalk buttons at thousands of intersections in New York have offered pedestrians false hope. The well-worn buttons offer proof that individuals believed the sign that says, "To Cross Street, Push Button." But according to a 2004 article in *The New York Times,* all this button pushing is futile. With the emergence of computer-controlled traffic signals, the city deactivated these buttons years ago, yet pedestrians stand there and impatiently push them day after

day without actually accomplishing anything.[1]

On the other hand, the buttons aren't causing any harm. In fact, it can be argued these buttons actually relieve some stress as the people feel they are doing something to help speed things up.

But it is important to understand that helping without discernment is different than standing at a crosswalk pushing a disconnected button. Pushing a dysfunctional button is neutral. It is neither doing good nor causing harm. But improper giving can be far different. Many times when we try to fix every problem by throwing money at it, we actually create greater problems. As Randy Alcorn once said, "it has the same effect as trying to put out a fire by throwing gasoline on it."[2]

Aiming at the Right Target (18)

It was Sunday morning of the 2004 Olympics, and as Matt Emmons prepared to compete, he had every reason to be confident. He already led by three points in the 50-meter rifle competition, and all he needed was a halfway decent shot. That three-point lead meant that if Matt could hit even close to the bull's-eye, the gold medal would be his. So as he got into position that morning, he felt no reason for concern. Even Matt's competitors knew they were outmatched. Matt came to Athens, Greece, that year with a string of victories behind him, and he had already won one Olympic gold medal there in a previous event. Matt had a reputation as a steady hand, and throughout these Olympics he had displayed the same calmness and accuracy in shooting that had made him famous in sport rifle competition.[1]

In these contests, competitors shoot at a target fifty meters away. Directly above each target is a number identifying the lane assigned to it. Matt was shooting in lane two, and as he prepared to shoot, his primary thought was to remain calm. Nerves are the enemy in competitive shooting. The bull's-eye on the target in this event is smaller than a dime, so even the slightest movement can destroy a shot. If a competitor can't control his emotions under pressure, he isn't well-fitted for the sport. But Matt had spent many hours preparing for this moment, and he felt calm and confident as he slowly squeezed the trigger.

Matt Emmons' shot that morning was nearly perfect. It hit the bull's-eye almost directly in the center, and without question, Matt was by far the best sharpshooter on the line that day. His gun performed perfectly, his aim had been good, and the bullet had gone exactly where Matt had aimed. The beautiful shot was good enough to secure his gold medal and send him home a winner, but there was one problem.

Matt had aimed at the wrong target.

Instead of aiming at the target in his own lane, Matt had accidently crossed over and focused on the target in lane three. It was a wonderful shot, but at the wrong target. In his determination to remain cool under stress, he had forgotten to glance at the lane number above the target.

"On that shot," he said later, "I was just worrying about calming myself down and just breaking a good shot, and so I didn't even look at the number."

Cross firing is an extremely rare mistake in elite competition, but the officials had no choice but to award Matt a score of zero. The gold medal went to another competitor who had not shot as well but who had focused on the right target.

In the last chapter we discussed Jim, the man whose need changed as time went on. While at first his need was money to cover his unexpected costs, later his real need was mentoring. Well-meaning people who continued sending him money did not recognize that the need had shifted. They focused, like Matt Emmons, on the wrong target.

This lesson is critical when helping others. You may have abundant resources and ability to help others. You may even have years of experience reaching out to those in need. Like Matt Emmons, you might have flawless motives and machinery. But if you have an improper focus, all that energy, effort, and experience may be misdirected.

Recently I was working with an overseas mission that was having trouble with continuous begging. They had started handing out a little aid when the situation seemed to warrant it, but as the years went by, they found themselves giving out more and more. Finally they realized they were in trouble. Much of the aid they were handing out dealt only with symptoms, and they suddenly had to face the facts. They had aimed at the wrong target.

"For twenty years," one of the administrators told me with regret, "we have tried to help these people, and now I am beginning to see that our 'help' was actually a major part of the problem." This mission discovered that their gifts of aid, given too freely, had kept the people from focusing on their own God-given resources. The mission had been shooting at symptoms rather than the cause.

Identifying the Correct Target

Identifying the correct target isn't always easy. When my wife and I were first married, we lived across the street from a church in a small town. Our part of town was not very affluent, and we frequently saw people who were obviously in a low-income bracket. We hadn't lived there long till we began to notice that when people had a need, they came to this church. Some of these needy people were just passing through town, but they stopped by, hoping to find someone who could help them with their problem. But since the church was small and didn't have anyone there during the day, sometimes they would walk over to our house to find help.

One young family began frequenting our doorstep. We were young, idealistic, and eager to help, so we began giving them what they asked for. After all, didn't Jesus say we should give to him who asks? I was usually at work when they came, so my wife needed to deal with these requests. At first they had stories of emergencies and needed cash on short notice, but as the frequency increased and the stories began to grow in creativity, we decided to stop giving cash. So we gave canned goods and various items they needed for themselves or their children out in the car. But finally I began to wonder if we were really blessing this family. The next time they came, my wife told them to come back on Saturday when I would be home. The husband came that next weekend needing groceries, and after some discussion, I went with him to the grocery store. We walked up and down the aisles purchasing what they needed, and I used the opportunity to suggest some job opportunities to him and to teach the importance of seriously searching for work. I also talked to him about the need to purchase only essential grocery items and discussed the difference between wants and needs. He didn't really appreciate this, and when I wouldn't buy a case of soft drinks (something our own budget couldn't afford) he obviously wasn't happy. We paid for the groceries, and I told him I would gladly help again, but the next time he came, I wanted to hear how his search for work was going.

That was the last we ever heard from the family, but I have thought of them often. Many of us have had experiences like this, and had I continued giving money or even food, the begging would probably have continued for a long time. Sometimes our primary goal is to get the beggar out of our path, and it seems easiest to give what he asks for. In this case, the real need wasn't food, diapers, or money for fuel or rent. The underlying problem was laziness and dependency. If I had continued to focus on symptoms, I may have harmed the very family I wanted to help.

Taking Time

When Matt Emmons later analyzed what had gone wrong during the 2004 Olympics, he realized his only error was not taking the time to look closely at where he was aiming. Most of us in North America live busy lives. We schedule our lives with calendars, timers, and day planners. Every event needs to neatly fit into a particular time slot, and we don't have much room for the unexpected. We even justify our hurried existence with Bible phrases like "redeeming the time" as we rush off to yet another social engagement.

Consequently, when someone suddenly appears on our horizon asking for help, we don't think we have time to investigate. But should we take time? The answer to this question goes back to the topic of motives, which we addressed in the beginning of the book. If our goal is to get the person out of the way so that we can get back to our tightly scheduled day, then perhaps we don't have time. But if we want to provide real help, it will require time. Time, for many of us, is our most precious resource. But it is also most needed, in every culture, if we are going to help effectively.

In 2002, King Mswati III of Swaziland traveled to various countries asking for aid. There was an obvious need in his country, where 65 percent of the population lives in abject poverty, and 33 percent are HIV positive. King Mswati III arrived in these other countries to beg for healthcare funds aboard a $45 million jet he had purchased that year. Many countries and organizations responded with aid, but if they had only taken a little time to research the situation, they would have discovered that the cost of King Mswati's jet was twice Swaziland's annual healthcare budget.[2] Trying to address the great need in Swaziland by giving money to King Mswati was probably misdirected. Just a little investigation would have revealed where funds were actually ending up.

The Aim of an Organization

Several years ago I had dinner with a Chinese lady in Beijing who worked for a large Christian mission. This mission was an outreach of a mainstream American Protestant denomination, and this woman had been employed by them for several years. She expressed her appreciation for the job she had and the income it provided. For many house church believers in China, jobs can be hard to find. But even though she was thankful for the income, she was a frustrated woman.

She told us that the only thing this organization seemed to care about was a slip of paper each month telling how many Chinese had been converted through the efforts of this organization. "It is so frustrating," she said with deep emotion. "There is so much here that needs to be done. But because the administration cares more about changed numbers than changed lives, we aren't accomplishing nearly what we could." She talked about the efforts she has made to talk to her American superiors, but it always comes back to the same thing. They need good numbers to continue getting good support.

> *Sometimes it is easier for an organization to demonstrate that their goals are being achieved than it is to prove that their goals are worth achieving.*

I left that meeting with a heavy heart. The needs are so great in China, and people so receptive. But if an organization begins aiming at changing numbers rather than changing lives, they are aiming at the wrong target. Regardless how well-oiled the machine is and how intently they focus, if it is the wrong goal, the effort will be in vain. This mission's misguided aim brings to mind Albert Einstein's quote,

"Not everything that can be counted counts, and not everything that counts can be counted." Sometimes it is easier for an organization to demonstrate that their goals are being achieved than it is to prove that their goals are worth achieving.

Conclusion

The story of Matt Emmons provides a sober reminder. Whether we are running an aid organization, called to be a deacon in the local church, or trying to help our struggling neighbor, we greatly need constant self-examination. All of us want to bless others. We have a desire to help people. But so often we find ourselves in a hurry, not taking the time to care, investigate, and examine our aim.

Sometimes, as in the story of Jim, the need changes. But other times we are the ones who change. We start out with a clear vision of the goal and how to reach it. The large Protestant mission probably began with a clear intention of presenting the Gospel and changing lives. They wanted to provide spiritual help to the Chinese people. But over time they became fixated on the needed income stream and the numbers that kept that stream alive. Just having ability, resources, and a desire to help is not enough. It is also imperative to aim at the right target.

Categorizing Need 19

So how can we determine the real need as we attempt to reach over the wall? How can I know what type of help is called for in a specific situation? As we look for answers to these questions, we want to break down material need into two basic categories. We will refer to one of these as critical need.

Critical Need

This need results from a calamity such as a house fire, earthquake, medical emergency, or tsunami, where people are suddenly thrust into desperate circumstances. Many times there are disastrous consequences if these needs are not met immediately. The earthquake in Haiti on January 12, 2010, is an excellent example. For the first few weeks after the event, people needed to be rescued from the debris. They urgently needed access to pure water, emergency medical care, food, and shelter. These people had no ability to help themselves. Many were pinned under rubble and would have died if someone hadn't rushed to their rescue.

Gerline Louissaint experienced the trauma of the Haiti earthquake. Sitting in front of her home in Port-au-Prince that afternoon, talking to her neighbors, Gerline was preparing to go inside to begin the evening meal for her family when the earthquake struck. Her house suddenly collapsed, with huge slabs of concrete falling over her and slamming her to the ground. When the shaking stopped, Gerline found herself buried under the wreckage of her home. She was completely powerless and at the mercy of rescue teams working in the area who finally found and uncovered her the next day. Gerline's experience is a good example of critical need. This event came upon her suddenly, and she had no way to take care of her needs. For weeks after that, she was dependent on others for medical care, purified water, and a supply of food. I listened as with tears she shared the tremendous blessing she had received from a few foreigners who helped her during this time of crisis. She saw the love of Jesus in them.

There are also people in the world who have not experienced a sudden calamity, yet fall into this category. It may be those with physical handicaps or mental disorders, and even the elderly who are no longer self-sufficient. They are in a precarious situation and need a specific type of aid. We will look more closely at critical need and how the Bible instructs us to deal with it in another chapter, but right now we want to simply understand what we are referring to when we speak of critical need.

Chronic Need

Other people living in poverty do not fall under the category of critical need. In fact, we could argue that most do not. Much poverty is ongoing. We can think of entire countries where they have adequate rainfall, plenty of land, and sufficient manpower, yet they have difficulty making things work. It seems they always struggle to feed and clothe their citizens. We refer to this as chronic need, and this is entirely different from critical need. In these situations the root cause of the need is harder to determine. When a family's house burns down, the root cause of their poverty is easy to identify. One day they were doing fine, and the next day they didn't have a roof over their heads. They had a sudden crisis, and it is easy to pinpoint the time and place it occurred.

But ongoing need is different. Daw Aye, the mother of a growing family, lives in a small village near the southern end of Myanmar. Just providing food for her children takes all her focus and energy. In addition to cooking food and taking care of laundry, Daw is also self-employed. Her business consists of buying and selling vegetables from a small table in front of her home.

Her entire sales display is about four feet long and two feet wide. When I visited her home in 2009, her entire business inventory consisted of one watermelon, two squash, and about fifteen fresh avocados. You don't need to walk in the door to take a tour of Daw's home. It is constructed of bamboo slats and covered with a thatched roof, and in daylight you can see completely through the house. There is no need to vacuum the carpet or mop the floor. All the houses in her village have dirt floors. Daw is one of millions in our world who constantly live on the ragged edge of survival.

But you couldn't go back in Daw's history and pinpoint a time when this poverty began. She grew up in a home similar to this one, and abject poverty is all she has ever known. She is able-bodied and works hard every day, yet her situation has continued to worsen year after year. Daw Aye is an example of chronic need.

We need to realize that not all need is as easy to categorize as the examples we have given. Properly identifying which kind of need we are dealing with takes prayerful discernment. And in addition to the difficulty in properly diagnosing each situation, another factor makes discernment even more difficult: almost everyone believes his own situation is critical need!

This Is a Crisis!

Recently I met with a small group of people in Ghana who were asking for help. These people obviously had resources and good health, so to me it seemed clear the need was chronic. I presented a plan in which they would begin saving small amounts of money until they had enough to begin small enterprises. When I had concluded, one of the ladies spoke up.

"Sir," she said in a disgusted tone, "you don't seem to understand. We are extremely poor here in Ghana. We don't have anything to save! Unless you first give us something to begin, we can never start a business."

I had implied that their situation was not critical and that they had resources they could use more efficiently. She was saying, "You have misdiagnosed our situation. This is critical, and we need a gift." But I was confident this situation was more a problem of management than of money, so I told them I would be glad to help set up a savings group, but nothing free would be given.

When they saw that no money would be handed out, they became interested in saving and started asking more questions. At the end of the meeting they began to visualize what they could accomplish as a group, and they became excited about starting to save. Before I left, the same woman who had said they had nothing to get started with offered me sixty dollars to help start a savings group! This money had been in her wallet even as she begged, but she first wanted to see if this American would give out gifts before she committed any of her own assets.

This scenario is common in developing countries. Some have received so many gifts over the years, they have come to expect more. But in situations like these, more gifts can compound the problem and prevent them from addressing their real need.

Conclusion

For too long, too many governments, organizations, churches, and well-meaning people have tried to treat all types of need the same way. But just imagine what would happen if a mother tried this with her children. Consider for a moment two scenarios. In the first, a four-year-old boy runs into the house crying. The mother asks him what is wrong, and between sobs he says his arm hurts. The mother continues to investigate and discovers he fell off his bike and landed on his arm. In the second scenario, a four-year-old boy again runs into the house crying. The mother asks him what is wrong, and between sobs he says his arm hurts. But the mother continues to investigate and discovers his father had told him to hoe the garden. He doesn't want to hoe and says that when he hoes, he gets tired and his arm hurts.

Notice, the external symptoms look the same. The child cries, runs to Mother, and says his arm hurts. But wouldn't most wise mothers respond differently after investigating? If the young boy had been hurt in an accident, she would probably hold him, comfort him for a moment, and maybe even tell him to lie down and rest. When a child is injured, he needs love and immediate affection. But the second scenario is completely different. A child who refuses to work does need attention, but probably a completely different kind—perhaps even a trip to the woodshed!

The importance of categorizing need is easy to understand in our homes, yet sometimes we forget how important it is to determine the real need when trying to help the poor. But make no mistake—it is no less crucial.

The Appropriate Response

J esus once told a story that has become so familiar, I often forget its significance. We call it the story of the Good Samaritan, and it tells of a sudden crisis and how others responded to it. As with many of the powerful illustrations Jesus used to drive his point home, we tend to get caught up in the details and forget the primary thrust of the story. Jesus had just told the people the importance of loving God and loving our neighbor, and one of the men standing by asked, "And who is my neighbour?"[a] The Bible says this lawyer asked this question in an attempt to justify himself. He wanted parameters. He knew, just as we do, that this teaching could make his life uncomfortable.

I don't know what the lawyer thought Jesus would do with his question. Maybe he thought Jesus would say anyone within a one-mile radius would qualify. Or maybe he assumed Jesus would keep it within the lawyer's own ethnic group. But Jesus told an account that probably made this lawyer wish he had learned the art of silence earlier in life. The story of the Good Samaritan eliminates boundaries and focuses on searching for ways to bless others. Jesus taught that loving our neighbor means looking for opportunities rather than excuses.

I see this as the primary lesson in this account, and we still have trouble adjusting to this view. This powerful illustration demolishes all our attempts at self-justification. It is life from Jesus' perspective. We have all listened to discussions among believers about local versus foreign need. And inevitably we begin to hear a certain word emerge repeatedly from the conversation: "responsibility." We want to know how much obligation we have for this situation over here, or how responsible we are to help in that crisis over there. Like the lawyer in the Bible,

---

[a] Luke 10:29

we want to know who our neighbor is.

But the Good Samaritan didn't see the situation as one where he was legally required to help. He saw opportunity. We should be hearing each other say, "Have you heard about this need over here? What a wonderful opportunity and an open door for ministry!" I believe that was the primary point of this lesson.

But there is another lesson we want to get from this illustration. As we have discussed the importance of discerning between two basic types of need, the account of the Good Samaritan provides a wonderful Biblical example of critical need. The Bible says a man was going down from Jerusalem to Jericho and was attacked by thieves who took his clothes, wounded him, and left him half dead. So there he lay on the road—alone, without clothes, and in great need of emergency medical care.

This traumatic event happened suddenly. The man had no resources to help himself and lay there on the road naked, wounded badly enough to be classified as half dead. Surely this would qualify as critical need. So what is the appropriate response?

Imagine the foolishness of walking up to this man lying on the road and offering a great teaching program or trying to instruct him about the benefits of saving money and eventually having enough to start his own little business. This man doesn't need teaching or access to some sustainability-oriented program. This man needs help, and he needs it now. The Bible says the Samaritan "had compassion on him, and went to him, and bound up his wounds, pouring in oil and wine, and set him on his own beast, and brought him to an inn, and took care of him."[b] Even beyond this, he gave instructions to the innkeeper for the wounded man's care and left money to cover the costs.

This Samaritan poured himself into the need without asking for anything in return. Remember, this Samaritan wasn't just out taking a stroll. He was already busy that day. He wouldn't have taken the risk of traveling down this dangerous road while carrying money unless he had a good reason. He needed to go someplace, and this man lying on the road was an inconvenience. But he set aside all those issues, focused on the need before him, and offered relief.

[b] Luke 10:33, 34

The Need for Relief

Relief is the appropriate response to critical need, and I see examples of this all around today. If a house fire occurs in our communities, I see brothers and sisters in Christ respond immediately. If a tornado touches down in some part of the country, I see men drop their occupations and drive or fly many miles to provide relief. Even in other parts of the globe, I have seen people who thought they didn't have any extra time suddenly walk away from all their pressing business cares to provide the appropriate relief. These were not believers trying to discern whether or not this is really their responsibility. They were seeing opportunity!

Sometimes these situations lead to wonderful opportunities to share the Gospel. After a natural disaster in countries like Indonesia, Pakistan, or Bangladesh, building projects have resulted in contacts, questions, and great opportunities. Some of these countries not normally friendly to Christian influence are much more open after a disaster. A small window opens for a short time where believers can come in and demonstrate the life of Jesus. If we neglect these windows that briefly appear and then are gone, we overlook wonderful opportunities. God was clear throughout the Bible. He cares about the widow, the orphan, and anyone else who is destitute and unable to take care of himself. Critical need calls for relief.

Several years ago I was in Nicaragua and had the opportunity to go on a food box distribution. We visited many widows, and I watched as boxes of food were carried to their little houses. Life is difficult in that country even if you are able-bodied. But for these helpless women, relief was a godsend. The grateful smiles spoke volumes about their appreciation to God and those who sent aid. A handicapped widow without family and unable to provide for herself is a good example of critical need.

The Need for Opportunity

But what is the appropriate response when the need is diagnosed as chronic? What does the Bible say regarding people who have ability but are still poor? Let's look at how God told the children of Israel to address this kind of need.

And when ye reap the harvest of your land, thou shalt not wholly reap the corners of thy field, neither shalt thou gather the gleanings of thy harvest. And thou shalt not glean thy vineyard, neither shalt thou gather every grape of thy vineyard; thou shalt leave them for the poor and the stranger: I am the Lord your God.[c]

Later on in the Law God gives even more detailed instructions.

When thou cuttest down thine harvest in thy field, and hast forgotten a sheaf in the field, thou shalt not go again to fetch it: it shall be for the stranger, for the fatherless, and for the widow: that the Lord thy God may bless thee in all the work of thine hands. When thou beatest thine olive tree, thou shalt not go over the boughs again: It shall be for the stranger, for the fatherless, and for the widow. When thou gatherest the grapes of thy vineyard, thou shalt not glean it afterward: it shall be for the stranger, for the fatherless, and for the widow.[d]

How do we know this was chronic need? Because the poor in this situation were obviously able to work. They were capable of working in the field, something the man lying on the Jericho road could not have done. The poor in this situation simply lacked opportunity.

Have you ever considered how difficult it would have been for the average Jew to live out these commands? Leave part of the harvest out in the field?! I suspect the average Jewish farmer was like most good businessmen, not known for ignoring potential profit. Most likely few commands in the Law were more difficult for the Jewish man at harvest than this one. But regardless, these passages and others like them provide insight into the heart of God.

- **God intended that we provide opportunity to those in ongoing poverty.** I see opportunity in the "corners of the field" teaching in the Law. The lazy man couldn't complain about hunger. Food was available, but he had to get out of bed to get it. Years ago I worked for a wealthy man who was always

---

[c] Leviticus 19: 9, 10

[d] Deuteronomy 24:19-21

complaining about the American welfare system. "There is no reason to keep sending out checks," he said. "Just shut off the aid, and they will find a job. Hunger is a wonderful motivator!" And while I didn't always appreciate his insensitivity to the plight of the poor, what he said had some truth, especially in developed countries like the United States. Many people in our welfare system would get out and find work if the checks would suddenly stop coming. Hunger does motivate. But many of the poor are in fact willing to work, yet they lack teaching, capital, and proper tools to be productive. God wants us to provide opportunity for them to provide for themselves.

- **God intended that the poor work.** In fact, He wanted them to work hard. He could have said, "Let them go into the field before you do and reap the choicest parts of the field." But He didn't say that. They were to glean after the farmer had finished harvesting the crop. I don't know just how many grapes and olives the average Jewish farmer left behind him, but I suspect they didn't leave any more than necessary. This process of gleaning probably wasn't easy, but God wanted the poor to work.

God isn't interested in programs that discourage a man from working. Paul told the church at Thessalonica, "For even when we were with you, this we commanded you, that if any would not work, neither should he eat."[e] Those are strong words. Were they to just stand by and watch a man die if he didn't get up and work? But notice, Paul doesn't say *couldn't* work, he says *wouldn't* work. There will always be some who cannot work. They are in critical need, and we addressed this earlier. But if a man will not work, this verse is saying you shouldn't feed him. This man needs to get up and work. Don't give him food—give him an opportunity to work.

This principle is just as true in foreign countries as in our

---

[e] 2 Thessalonians 3:10

local communities. If a man doesn't want to work but we keep giving him food, we are disobeying this important teaching. Many times our inclination is to harvest the crop, process it for him, and then set the ready-to-eat meal on his doorstep. In our great sympathy for the plight of the poor, we tend to respond in ways that are really not Biblical. God intends that every able-bodied individual be productive and work to provide for himself and his family.

- **Even the widow and the fatherless were to work.** These Scriptures show clearly that just being a widow or an orphan does not automatically exempt one from work. The determining factor is whether or not the person is capable. The Apostle Paul addressed this issue as well in his letter to Timothy. The early church provided for the widows, but Paul told them certain qualifications should be met before the church would begin providing. Paul was saying they shouldn't start providing for a woman just because she was a widow. Her family should be called on so that the church could focus assistance on those who were actually without support, resources, or ability to provide for themselves.[f] Many widows, even in poor countries, are able to provide for themselves. They may need some capital, encouragement, and teaching, but they are capable of making an income on their own. Just because they are widows doesn't mean they are helpless.

> *The surest way to create long-term problems is to begin providing free food to a man who won't work.*

These Scriptures demonstrate clearly that the appropriate response in these situations is not relief but opportunity. If a man can't provide for himself because he is ignorant, provide teaching. If he knows how to work but lacks capital, you may need to help him obtain funding.

---

[f] 1 Timothy 5: 3-16

If he lacks confidence and has never had a good role model, you may need to walk beside him and encourage him. But remember, don't do anything for him that he can do himself. The surest way to create long-term problems is to begin providing free food to a man who won't work.

Conclusion

I don't intend to imply that each scenario we confront will be easy. We won't always do it right. I have never met anyone involved very long in poverty relief who still believes he always diagnoses every situation properly. Helping can be humbling. But don't let the complexity of assisting the poor discourage you. God gave us these principles to use and apply. He has a heart for those in need, and if we want to effectively help the poor, we have to understand and apply these basic principles.

There is a time to just dump out aid, forget the cost, and freely give. This is how Jesus responded to our need. Like the man on the Jericho road, we were hopeless and helpless. We had critical need. "But God, who is rich in mercy, for his great love wherewith he loved us, Even when we were dead in sins, hath quickened us together with Christ, (by grace ye are saved.)"[g] Like the Good Samaritan, Jesus came and freely poured in relief. There are times when He calls us to do the same.

But there are also more complex situations. When faced with ongoing and even multi-generational poverty, a solution is not quite so simple. Knowing how to provide opportunities in these cases will take humility, patience, and prayerful discernment.

---

[g] Ephesians 2:4, 5

How Can I Know?

W hen that stranger rings the doorbell, when a brother in our congregation has a financial need, or when we travel to an impoverished country, how can we know what kind of need we are dealing with? In this chapter we want to put work clothes on the Biblical principles we have looked at. We want to look at some steps we can take to make sure we are actually helping the person with the need.

As we begin, let's look at some questions we should ask as we attempt to categorize the need and provide the appropriate response. Remember, it will take more than just finding the answer to one of these questions to evaluate the need. Yet each answer provides an important clue and will help to properly diagnose the problem.

Clue 1: Did the situation happen suddenly? Is the need you are trying to address the result of a sudden calamity? Did some unexpected external force like an earthquake, tornado, or sickness bring on the need? Remember the example of the man going down from Jerusalem to Jericho. He was doing fine until the bandits robbed and beat him. If you can identify the day the problem began, you have your first clue. You are probably dealing with critical need, and the appropriate response would be relief. Time is usually crucial here, and the sooner you can get aid to the individual, the better. But if this need did not originate suddenly, you are almost always facing chronic need. In this case move slowly, asking questions and taking time to determine how to best address the situation.

Clue 2: Do they lack physical or mental ability? This question is essential. If they are not physically or mentally capable of addressing their situation, it is critical need and calls for relief. This doesn't always mean you are the one who should provide the aid, as we will address later, but the answer to this question does define the type of aid needed. God cares about those who are not able to care for themselves, and He wants us to care for them as well. Many times these people get neglected because they have nothing to offer us. But it is imperative to reach out to the helpless just as God reached out to us.

Clue 3: Will they be harmed if I do nothing? This is an important and often neglected question. If you just ignored the situation, would the person die? Would he bleed to death? Now make no mistake, we are not insinuating that doing nothing is the correct response. Rather, we are trying to identify the type of need we are facing and what response it calls for. If nothing terrible would happen, then you are probably dealing with chronic need. But if, like the man on the Jericho road, the person is half dead and ignoring him would cause irreparable harm, you are looking at critical need.

This question is especially significant in developing countries. Too often we walk into poor villages and assume things need to change immediately. The level of poverty is much worse than anything we have ever known, and we decide something must change today. But in almost all those places, even if you don't do anything, no one will die. They do have need, but if you choose to provide imme-diate relief, quite likely you will only make the problem worse.

Clue 4: Do they lack basic resources? The answer to this question also provides an important clue to the type of need. But this one isn't always as easy to discern as we might think. Many times we tend to underestimate the poor. Sylvester in Ghana is an example of this. Blinded in an accident, one would assume Sylvester would certainly be a prime candidate for ongoing relief. But instead, Sylvester was deter-mined to find a way to provide for his family. He took some training, found some used equipment, and received a small loan to get started. Using this, Sylvester created a thriving soap-making business, producing over five hundred bars of soap a week to provide a good income for his family.

We tend to assume a blind man needs someone to provide for him, but Sylvester had resources. He had a supportive family, strong determination, and physical ability to make soap. Just some teaching and capital provided the opportunity Sylvester needed. Taking time to research often shows that the needy have more God-given ability and resources than we first assumed.

Clue 5: Were they using good management skills? Remember, we are looking for clues about the type of need and the appropriate solution. This question is important, not because we want to punish someone for poor choices, but because it is critical to make sure we work on the problem and not just a symptom. If you mistakenly provide just relief, you might only relieve symptoms and shield people from the consequences of their mistakes. In this case you may inadvertently set them up for continued problems. Each of us needs to learn from our mistakes, and we are not helping someone if we constantly protect him from the results of poor decisions.

> *We are not helping someone if we constantly protect him from the results of poor decisions.*

Clue 6: Is this the first attempt to help? Take time to investigate whether or not the individual has been receiving help from others. Many times the appropriate cure includes cutting off ongoing aid. But sometimes when a benefactor finally turns the aid spigot off, the needy person just moves over to a different doorstep. In many of our conservative circles, a man who becomes accustomed to begging can exist for years due to the size of the donor base. This is where our deacons should take responsibility. A deacon should be aware of the needs in his congregation, and those of us who receive requests for help should communicate with him before providing aid.

Of course, for this to work, the deacon must take his role seriously. He should be able to discern whether the need is critical or chronic. He should be ready to either sit down and provide financial teaching himself or delegate someone in the congregation to do it. If we can equip our deacons and use this Biblical model, we will be in a better position to provide real help in our congregations.

This also calls for good communication between fellowships. In our eagerness to receive someone leaving another fellowship, we need to communicate with the church that person is leaving. Did this man have good relationships in the congregation he is coming from? Is he trying to walk away from accountability?

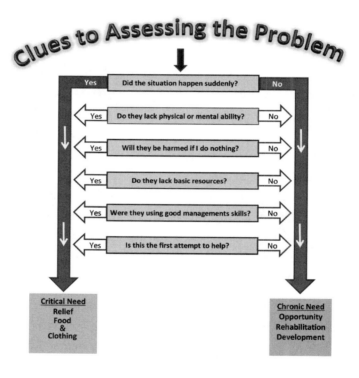

This question should be asked in foreign countries as well. Are other organizations already working in this community? Many of the needy become adept at manipulating aid organizations. But taking time to find the answer to this question can help you determine what kind of problem you are addressing. If they have received aid for this problem from someone else in the past, there is a good possibility you are dealing with chronic need.

Considering the Clues

It would be nice if we could just ask one question and the answer would clearly define what type of need we are working with. But proper discernment isn't always easy. Each of these clues holds some weight, yet none is the only clue needed. To illustrate this, let's take these clues and apply them to an exaggerated hypothetical situation.

Imagine you have a neighbor who has always struggled financially. He has a good-paying job, yet his money is quickly spent. He likes to enjoy the latest gizmos and gadgets, but somehow never gets around to maintaining his house. You watch as year after year this man's house deteriorates. Finally one day, while his family is gone, the house collapses during a storm. So when your neighbor returns home, he heads over to your house, rings the doorbell, and asks for help.

If you used only Clue 1 to determine whether this man needs a handout, you would conclude that you should write him a check. This calamity happened suddenly. A storm came, the wind blew his house down, and he needs immediate relief. But if you would continue down the list, you would arrive at a completely different conclusion. Clue 5 would suggest that if he hadn't been maintaining his house, just giving him another one might not address his real need. Maybe your neighbor's real need is someone to walk beside him and help him develop his management skills. One author said, "One of the biggest mistakes that North American churches make—by far—is applying relief in situations in which rehabilitation or development is the appropriate intervention."[1]

Working With and Through the Community

Another issue we neglect many times has to do with how we administer help in underdeveloped settings. We ask all the right questions and become certain that a situation is critical need. We may be right. But in our haste to provide relief, we forget to use the local church or community. Just because we have the resources, and all the clues point to critical need, doesn't mean we are the ones to administer the aid.

Many organizations have programs that sponsor children, students, or families, but they do not work through the local community. Then when faced with a sudden calamity, they wonder why the nationals run to the missionaries rather than look for solutions themselves. When the organization is suddenly forced to leave the country, the local people do not know how to take care of themselves. They have learned to rely on that hot meal every day and have never learned to provide

> *It is better to provide opportunity for the church to take care of its own than to just give relief and render the church powerless.*

for themselves. This is why teaching should always be part of the solution and part of our programs. Though many of these communities appear poor to us, they could support their own schools, widows, and orphans as the Scriptures instruct if someone would walk beside them and help the church teach its own people. We can do great damage when we bypass their God-given structures and provide relief without considering the place of teaching the teachers within the local church and community.

This principle is true in your local congregations as well. If you decide it is a critical situation, make sure the local church is part of your solution. It will take more time, but it is better to provide opportunity for the church to take care of its own than to just give relief and render the church powerless.

Conclusion

Louissaint Louime pastors a small church in rural Haiti. He is a small, smiling man with whitening hair, and like most men in his village, he is at work before dawn. Like many rural Haitians, Louissaint isn't really sure how old he is. A journalist from the Associated Press interviewed Louissaint several years ago, and the resulting article described the need for discernment in Haiti.

Louissaint's congregation is often without food, and they live in huts made of cornstalks. But in spite of the poverty he has experienced during his lifetime, more aid is not what Louissaint longs for. He has watched as foreigners drive their trucks through his village, throwing out food and clothing as they go. "People close to the trucks grab as much as they can and sell it later," Louissaint said, "but everyone else gets nothing, and there is no lasting benefit."[2]

What Louissaint would really like is someone to come and teach people in his congregation better farming techniques, or someone to start a small microfinance program to help his young men get started in business. He would like to see people come who would teach skills, instead of just making themselves feel better by giving away stuff they didn't need anyway.

Notice the underlying message from this experienced Haitian pastor. His people don't need more relief; they need opportunity. His village isn't dealing with a crisis; they are struggling with ongoing poverty. And until we begin taking the time to thoroughly investigate before helping, we will continue to misdiagnose and fail to properly address the real need.

The Curse of Dependency (22)

D emo Hassan[1] is a frustrated man. Demo works as a livestock trader in the city of Garbatulla in northern Kenya, and he has become concerned for his people. Demo is familiar with drought, famine, and political insecurity. He has been through the panic, violence, and social upheaval that accompany a widespread food shortage. But the reason for Demo's concern is something different. He is alarmed about what aid is doing to his people.

For years, truckloads of food and relief have poured into this region. The aid began after a famine in the 1960s, but today, several million people there receive regular shipments of aid whether it rains or not. Make no mistake—Demo is not against aid. He remembers a time when relief saved their lives.

"It was justified," says Demo, "because it helped desperate families who had lost their animals, their source of livelihood."

Now things have changed, and the people could support themselves, but they depend on aid instead. No longer is their greatest enemy drought, famine, or invading armies. Their greatest problem is now aid itself. Like a drug addict who cannot get along without another fix, many of these people are addicted to foreign aid. Demo continues his story:

> I often get sad when I see trucks loaded with free food. The free food has encouraged laziness; people just wait for the food rations. The youth, energetic men and women, who used to engage in livestock trade, work as herders, do crop farming and small businesses like selling milk and animals, have all abandoned their work [to] idle around and wait for free food. Free

food has dignified the habit of begging. It is common to see able-bodied men visiting NGOs (Non-Government Organizations) and government offices to beg for relief food, yet they could feed themselves and their families, do manual work, farm, or form a group to borrow money to start a small business. I am worried about our children dropping out of school to join their parents in waiting for relief food.

Dependency

In this chapter we want to look at the curse of dependency. How can aid end up harming the very people we are trying to help? How can a semi load of free food have the capability to save a community during a famine, yet have the ability to destroy them after the

famine? In the first chapter we looked at the great inequalities in our world. Some of us have more than we need. Like those lepers outside the wall of Samaria, we have more food than we can eat and have trouble storing all our possessions. But just over the wall, people have very little. Many are hungry, lack adequate healthcare, and struggle with substandard housing. The obvious response? Begin giving our excess to those who have need.

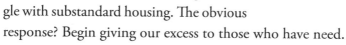

But after listening to the frustrations of community leaders like Demo Hassan, it is obvious that continuing to give can have negative consequences. So what should we do? Let's begin by considering the problem first, and then look at some steps we can take to help people avoid dependency and addiction to aid.

In the last several chapters we looked at various needs and the importance of determining which kind we are working with. We have also discussed that the appropriate response to each of these needs varies and we tend to do what is easiest. Since providing immediate relief is usually the easiest, this can become our default mode.

The Cause

Providing continued relief to lingering poverty is one of the chief causes of dependency. In Demo's area, there was a time when they were in the middle of a famine and the people had no way to provide for themselves. This was critical need, and the appropriate response was to send truckloads of food. But this relief should have been viewed as a short-term response. As soon as the crisis was over, the gifts should have stopped. The need had changed, and the people now needed opportunity rather than relief. The timing of this transition takes discernment, but to avoid creating dependency, this shift must occur.

Why is this transition so vital? Imagine for a moment that your nineteen-year-old son is sick. He came home from work with a high fever and complained of dizziness and a throbbing head. When you go into his room to check on him, he says he is hungry and would like some lunch. What kind of need is this? It is critical need. He is obviously not feeling well, and it would be a very hardhearted parent who would deny his request.

But let's imagine he continues to lie there for a week. His fever is gone, he acts normal again, and he spends his day reading books, but he still wants his meals delivered to his bed. How long would you keep providing room service? If you would continue bringing him food, you would be in great danger of creating dependency.

We need to understand that this principle is universal. When we continue to provide food, clothes, or shelter to people capable of providing for themselves, we sow the seeds of dependency, and we share in the blame for their condition. Most of us understand this concept in developed countries. We would not continue to feed an able-bodied son in bed or continue paying credit card bills for a brother who habitually makes poor choices. But when we go to underdeveloped countries, we tend to believe this principle doesn't apply. We compare their living conditions to our own and decide that continual relief is not only easier, it is also proper. We understand that welfare programs destroy incentive in our culture, but there is something else we need to understand: welfare doesn't work in theirs either.

A Mirror for the Poor

Earlier we said to beware what you think about the poor. This is so important it needs to be said again. What you think of the people you are trying to help will become their impression of themselves. If you see them as children of God, people with God-given abilities and gifts, they will begin to see themselves the same way. But if you see them as having little ability or resources, they will begin to see themselves the same way. Why is this?

It's simple. If you believe they are helpless, it will affect how you respond. You will continue to provide relief, and every time they receive another gift, they are reminded of their "inability" to provide for themselves. This is one of the detrimental impacts of long-term relief. It repeatedly drives home your belief in their worthlessness. And if you do this long enough, recovery is very difficult.

When working with microfinance in Haiti, I learned early on that people will struggle if they live near a town or along a main road. At first I couldn't understand why. The best place to operate a business is in town or beside main roads where the customer base is largest. So why did these people have more trouble repaying loans than those up in the mountains where poverty was much worse? The answer gradually became clear: those living along main roads have received much more aid over the years. Missionaries and aid organizations tend to help those easiest to access, so there is much more relief given out along these roads. Consequently, these people came to view themselves as very needy and unable to provide. In our response to their need, they develop a picture of who they are and whether or not they can provide for their own needs. Our response to their need becomes a mirror.

Hurting Versus Harming

Another problem in this cycle of dependency is our fear of hurting people. Several years ago I met with a group of microloan recipients who expected us to just ignore their unpaid business loans. Their community had received so much aid through the years that the citizens had come to expect continual relief when things got tough. I tried to remind them of their resources and abilities. I also told them we would not ignore their failure to repay simply because they were having difficulty.

This caused quite a stir in the group, and one man in the back stood up and began venting his frustration. "You call yourself a Christian," he said angrily. "You come from America where there is plenty, and we have children who need food and clothes. If you were really a Christian, you would give us what we need!"

I remember that day clearly, and I left that meeting feeling miserable. This man did have real needs. He did have children and was having difficulty providing for them. I knew all this. But I also knew that giving this man yet another gift would have harmed him. There is a big difference between hurting a man and harming him. When you go to the dentist and he fills a cavity, you expect it to hurt. That is just part of going to a dentist. But we don't expect a dentist to harm us. When I told the man I would not give him a gift, I knew I hurt him—but I didn't want to harm him.

Much dependency results from not distinguishing between hurting and harming. We are so afraid of hurting people. They are already poor, and we fear that saying no will hurt them more. But when we deal with ongoing poverty, we need to focus on not harming, rather than not hurting. When you refuse to keep delivering food to the bedside of your nineteen-year-old, it may hurt his feelings. If you have provided room service for a long time, he might even pout or become angry. But the ramifications of continuing room service are huge. You can destroy him by continuing to bring him food, and the long-term consequences are too great to ignore. If we become obsessed with not hurting the feelings of the poor, the potential for serious harm is real.

The Need for Local Buy-In

As individuals, organizations, and governments have seen the destructive nature of ongoing relief, many attempts have been made to help people become sustainable. But providing opportunity is not easy. Millions of dollars have been spent to equip people in chronic poverty with better tools, machinery, and food-processing equipment. Surely, the argument goes, if we give them the tools they lack, this will take care of their situation. But until the local people buy into a concept, little will be accomplished, and many of these programs have produced less than satisfactory results.

Roland Bunch, in his book *Two Ears of Corn,* gives his own testimony of observing these unsuccessful attempts.

> The rusting hulks of well-intentioned but long-forgotten giveaways are scattered all over the Third World. I have personally seen tractors by the dozens, not to mention ploughs, cultivators, generators, threshers, pumps, scythes, lanterns, and grain mills that were never repaired after the first time they broke down. There are donated granaries that were never used, free high-yield seed that was eaten, give-away breeding animals that were sold or slaughtered for meat, and forest and fruit tree seedlings that died while still sitting in their plastic bags. Villagers themselves usually recognize the uselessness of giving things away. Folk sayings in dozens of countries admit that people don't take care of things they never had to work for.[2]

All these gifts were given with the best of intentions. But if people living in poverty have never worked for what they receive and never bought into the project, these projects can become just another form of relief. When you give a man a piece of machinery and three months later a wheel falls off, he will probably call and tell you to come fix "your" machinery. So how can we avoid this? How can we provide real opportunity and long-term blessing in chronic poverty?

- **Make sure they are part of the initial planning.** This one is hard for us, but the recipient needs to help with the preliminary planning whenever possible. We tend to go in and impose our solutions on their problems. What is the end result? They assume that if the solution is yours, the problem must be yours as well. But if they help analyze the problem and find a solution, they are better prepared to repair equipment and keep looking for better solutions to "their" problems. This takes time, but for a project to be successful, the local people need to feel the weight of the responsibility for their situation from the beginning. This is not only because of our need for their buy-in. It is also because we need their input. As a development worker once said, "We must listen to them as if they have something to contribute, because they do."[3]

- **Solutions must cost them something.** When dealing with ongoing need, the one being blessed needs to bear the majority of the burden. Effective help provides what they can't, but never what they can. This is difficult because we assume there is little they can do. But search for ways they can repay what they receive. This not only helps them believe they are capable, it also teaches them to give back to their own community.

> *Effective help provides what they can't, but never what they can.*

- **Failure must have consequences.** When working with chronic need, every solution must cost the recipient something if it fails. If programs can fail without costing those involved, they probably will fail. Fear of failure is a wonderful motivator. When we remove that and insulate a person from all cost, we ask for failure. As soon as anyone learns, whether locally or in a foreign country, that you will pick up the tab if things don't work out, then be prepared to start picking up tabs. If a program is to be truly sustainable, it can't depend solely on us.

Conclusion

Relief is almost always the easiest short-term solution. We like to fix things fast, and sustainable solutions take time—sometimes a lot of time. But there are no shortcuts to sustainability. Many times in poverty, people have developed improper life patterns and habits that need to be changed. People become astute at begging but neglect their abilities and resources. Changing this pattern will take teaching and time, but the potential results are worth striving for. Continuing to give gifts will only delay this process.

In Kenya, Demo Hassan has started a campaign in his community called "Stop Free Food." He isn't asking that all aid stops. They do have great need. But he is requesting that organizations begin providing solutions that provide long-term help. "We can start by planning and identifying the talents of the [food aid] recipients," he said when interviewed. "Why should they be given free food permanently? We have many livestock traders like me who can be assisted with funds to purchase large herds of animals, hire trucks, and sell them to far-away, profitable markets in Nairobi [the capital] and other towns. Many families can resume crop farming. All they need is seeds and water pipes to supply water by gravity from the permanent rivers."[4]

This is coming from a man who wants the best for his country. He recognizes they need help. But Demo is looking for help that doesn't further harm his people. He is wise enough to see that they don't need more free aid. They need opportunity.

PART
FIVE

*Discovering
and Developing
What God Has
Given Them*

What Is in Your Hand? (23)

Katherine Williams and her husband were missionaries in the small state of Mizoram, India, during the early 1900s, and if there was ever a place that appeared to need foreign aid, Mizoram was that place. Mizoram lacked raw materials for manufacturing, and most of its citizens were subsistence farmers. Even to this day, Mizoram is known as one of India's least-developed states, and its people are considered the poorest of the poor. But Katherine and her husband had a strong desire to help these impoverished people become self-sustaining.

So Katherine began to set aside one handful of uncooked rice at each meal. She then sold it at the end of the week to support an evangelist in the area. Then she began teaching the women in the church to do the same. Rice was something they all had, so day by day, as the women prepared a meal, they would take one handful of rice, put it in a separate container, and save it for the work of evangelism. Every Sunday as they gathered for services, they brought this rice and dumped it into a container. The rice was then sold the next week in the local market, and the money used to buy literature and help support those who continued reaching out to others. Their congregation grew, and as more families came to the faith, more wives began saving a handful of rice at each meal.

This process of setting aside in Mizoram, India, known as *Buhfai Tham*, or *A Handful of Rice*, began in 1910, and for over one hundred years this tradition has continued. At first this method of saving for the Lord's work seemed insignificant. The first year the total value of all the rice donated was about $1.50. But over the years, the people have learned the value of giving and the blessing of sustainable outreach. In 2010, over $1,500,000 was donated through the *Buhfai Tham* savings plan.

Some who had other commodities began bringing what they could contribute. Today, some bring vegetables they have grown or firewood they have cut, and still others bring cash. Streaming out of communities each Sunday morning, they walk down the road to services carrying offerings they joyfully contribute to the Lord. These offerings are then taken to the local market, sold at a 50 percent discount to the extremely poor, and the proceeds used to fund the Lord's work. These people meet in church buildings they have paid for themselves and send out missionaries funded by these offerings. In fact, the church in Mizoram, India, has no interest in foreign aid. Even though the Mizo people have an average income of less than $1 per day, they have found blessing in giving of the resources the Lord has placed in their hands.[1] Like the churches in Macedonia, the church in Mizoram has learned the blessing of giving, even in deep poverty.[a]

> *When working with the poor, we must start with a focus on what they have, rather than what they lack.*

I often think of the believers in Mizoram, India. I am reminded of them when I hear young families say they just don't make enough to give. With the high cost of house, vehicle, and boat payments, they say, there isn't much left over. I also think of their story when I hear of missions that do not believe sustainability is possible where they are serving. Yet many of these missions are located in countries where the average income is ten times the income in Mizoram, India.

In this chapter we want to look at a basic principle essential to sustainability, whether locally or in a foreign country. The true story of the church in Mizoram underscores this basic principle. When working with the poor, we must start with a focus on what they *have,* rather than what they *lack.*

When a family has financial difficulty in America, it is almost always because they have focused on what they lack rather than the blessings they enjoy. We understand this. Yet when most of us walk into a poor

[a] 2 Corinthians 8:1, 2

foreign village for the first time, we neglect to see the potential there. We fail to notice that many things are working. We don't notice their natural resources and the abilities of the local people. Instead, we zero in on what they lack.

As we ask the local people about their needs, we also make them more conscious of all the things they don't have. Suddenly they become aware that they lack many things, some of which they may never before have heard of. This adds to their feelings of worthlessness and inferiority. But Katherine Williams didn't do this. She started with a basic belief that these people had resources (everyone had a little rice) that could be used to meet the needs of others and help spread the Gospel. What could they do with what the Lord placed in their hands?

There is a time to examine need and discover what kind of help is appropriate. But once we decide an individual or community is struggling with chronic poverty, it is time to begin looking for assets. Our role should be to help them uncover more of those assets and discover their opportunities. Many times, as in Katherine Williams' situation, the great need is teaching on better ways to use the opportunities they have.

In his book, *Walking With the Poor,* Bryant Myers labeled this starting-with-their-assets type of investigation *Appreciative Inquiry.* "Instead of looking for what is wrong or missing and then developing problem-solving responses," he says, "it looks for what is working, successful, and life-giving, and attempts to see additional possibilities."[2]

Several years ago I traveled with a pastor back a long, bumpy road in Central America to visit a small indigenous Mennonite church. The pastor was asking for help for this congregation, and it was obvious they were struggling with poverty. Several of the men in the area had left their families behind and had gone in search of jobs. The Sunday I was there, one of these men stood up after church and confessed sin in his life. He had fled the area trying to find work, found a job in America, and then in his loneliness had fallen into sin. He had returned now and repented, but other men had left their families and never returned.

This area is known for producing good coffee, yet the prices are so low that at times it is hardly worth harvesting. These men were willing to work, but in their setting a man could work hard day after day and have little to show for it. This pastor was looking for help.

How would you respond to a situation like this? These problems are not easy to solve, but let's go back to our first question. Is this critical or chronic need? Did this situation happen suddenly? No, this poverty developed over a long period of time. If you go through the rest of the questions outlined in chapter twenty-one, you will find this a classic case of chronic need.

Now if you would begin by analyzing their needs, you could create an impressive list. There are around sixty homes in this community and only one pickup truck. That seems like a definite need. They have muddy roads (almost impassable at times), no sewer system, substandard houses (many with dirt floors), no medical clinic, not an electric pole in sight, and little good clothing. This is the way we typically see a village like this, isn't it? Many needs! The typical response to needs like this is to start bringing in sea container loads of all the things we have decided they lack.

But the pastor who took me back there was too wise for this. He has lived in Central America long enough to see villages (and churches) destroyed by gifts. He was asking for a sustainable solution, so we began by making a list of their assets. First of all, they had healthy men who were willing to work. They also had the ability to grow high quality coffee. Both of these are great assets. In some North American communities, you can't find men willing to work hard for long hours. So we began looking at why the resources they had were not providing for their families as they should. Most of the problem was a lack of education on how coffee should be processed, insufficient capital to dry the coffee properly, and no access to good markets.

Consequently, connections were made with American businessmen who were willing to provide good teaching. In exchange, this community would provide a consistent supply of high quality coffee that would sell at a much better and more stable price. They were also taught how to form a co-op, and the co-op was able to then apply for a small loan to purchase a coffee dryer. This is a win-win, market-based business approach. These Central American farmers have incentive to work hard, and if they follow the teaching given to them, they will be able to provide good income for their families. They are also learning how to better manage their resources and work together as a community. By thinking and planning together, this community has developed some creative ways of pre-drying their coffee. But the burden was put on their shoulders, and this is their project.

If we are going to move people out of poverty without creating ongoing dependency, we need to start by focusing on their assets. This takes patience, long-term vision, and enough humility to allow them to become part of the solution.

In his book, *The Poor Will Be Glad*, Peter Greer tells of a man in Rwanda named Jean. After the genocide in Rwanda, many Christian organizations wanted to help rebuild this shattered country. Churches in America sent food and supplies and tried to help in various ways. As soon as things calmed down after the slaughter, Jean saw a need for eggs and decided to start a poultry business. He started small, scraping together funds to purchase a few chickens. But shortly after Jean had started marketing eggs, a church in America "adopted" the village where Jean lived and decided to donate free food and clothes to help these people. They went to a neighboring city and purchased eggs, brought them back and gave them to the villagers, and suddenly Jean's village was flooded with free eggs.

Of course, it isn't hard to guess what happened to Jean's egg business. His customers all disappeared, and Jean was forced to sell the chickens he had bought to support his family. One year after Jean sold his chickens, the church that had been supplying the free eggs turned their attention to another disaster in another part of the world, and now there was no one in his village who had layer chickens. Consequently, his village had to start buying eggs at a higher price than Jean had been charging before the "help" had arrived. The end result was that both Jean and his village were harmed economically by the good intentions of the American church.[3]

What is the lesson in this? Should the American church have stayed out of it? Absolutely not! Those Rwandans had—and still have—tremendous needs. If a man turns his back on the needs around the globe, then the Apostle John has a question: "How dwelleth the love of God in him?"[b] The love of God will constrain a believer to help, but couldn't we help a little smarter? Couldn't that church have started by looking for existing resources within that village instead of seeing only needs? Jean the chicken farmer would have been a wonderful resource for that church. With a small loan, he could have increased his production. This would have enabled Jean to produce a sustainable income for his family as well as bless his community for years to come.

To begin by looking for assets is not a denial that the poor have needs. Rather, it helps ensure that we are introducing long-term solutions. As one author said, "When considering bringing in outside resources, we must always ask two questions: 1) Is it too much? 2) Is it too early? It would be far better to let nonemergency need go unmet than to meet that need with outside resources and cripple the local initiative in the process."[4]

Sometimes locating assets in an area is difficult. Some of these impoverished places look nothing like the environment we are used to, and we long to instantly bring the tools, ideas, materials, and products we are familiar with. But these communities do have ways and methods they are familiar with. And the more we can integrate their tools, ideas, materials, and products into each project, the more sustainable it will become.

Conclusion

Most of us are not only fixers, but we like to fix things fast. Usually this consists of attempting to fix all the needs we see with products and manpower from home. Used to a quick-fix model, we have difficulty appreciating small steps. They seem so slow and insignificant.

I am sure when Katherine Williams first started teaching those women in India to set aside one handful of rice at a time, it must have seemed insignificant. But she started a tradition and taught a self-sustaining mindset that has blessed this region for over one hundred years. Insignificant as it may have seemed, it was done God's way, and He blessed it. As one of the national believers in Mizoram, India, recently said, "There are many ways of serving the Lord. Some people do great things.

---

[b] 1 John 3:17

Some people are good preachers, and some give lots and lots of money. But when we talk about this 'Handfuls of Rice,' it is very humble. The service is done in the corner of the kitchen where nobody sees. But God knows and He blesses it."[5]

THE OTHER SIDE OF THE WALL

Indigenous Sustainability (24)

M ost countries have some history they wish could be rewritten, periods when the events were traumatic and the memory brings fresh pain. For those who live in Bundibugyo in the western part of Uganda, the late 1990s is one of those times. Bundibugyo experienced outbursts of fighting between 1997 and 2000, and in 2001, members of the ADF (Allied Democratic Forces) came through Bundibugyo in a massive raid. Thousands of children were orphaned, and tens of thousands of citizens fled the area in fear. Those who fled were forced into refugee camps with terrible conditions. Lonely children didn't know where their families were, the facilities were filthy, and the refugees had little hope for the future. There wasn't enough food in these camps, and children went hungry for days at a time. The water supply was poor, many people had medical needs, and many began to die.

But in this camp was a man named Hannington Bahemuka. Like everyone else, Hannington lived in deplorable conditions where he lacked food and struggled to find sufficient water. Surviving this traumatic disaster seemed impossible. But in the face of this adversity, Hannington had something the others lacked. And ultimately, what Hannington possessed made all the difference.

Hannington was bishop of the local church in Bundibugyo, and he had a strong desire to help his people both physically and spiritually. Just before the war ravaged his home area, he had attended a seminar by an American organization encouraging local sustainability. He had learned that God owns and sustains everything and has given us resources wherever we live. It is our responsibility as good stewards to look for those resources and put them to work.

Hannington was also taught the importance of giving. Even though you may have only two mites, he was told, God wants us to enjoy the blessing of generosity. As Hannington lay down in his hastily constructed hut each night in that squalid refugee camp, he began to remember the teaching he had received. Were those Biblical principles really true? Could they work in any situation, even in a refugee camp? The people didn't have enough to eat, and they lacked clean water. How could he begin to teach them the principles of sustainability and the importance of giving?

So he began to pray, "Lord, how can I help my people out of this situation? What can I do?" Hannington decided to begin applying these principles and see what God would do. He started gathering the people in the camp regularly and shared the importance of believing that God owns and sustains everything. He also encouraged them to begin giving.

This wasn't easy for the people to accept, and many of them thought it was a waste of time. It seemed more important to put their energy into petitioning organizations in the West for help. Some were used to sponsorships and receiving aid from others. This concept of looking to their own people and resources for help sounded strange. But Hannington continued to teach, and the people gradually began to respond. Those who had two blankets found an orphan in the camp who didn't have any. When someone had access to extra food or water, instead of hoarding it, they began looking for someone who needed it more. Gradually, these refugees began to detect a different spirit in the camp.

One orphan girl who received an extra blanket later told of the impact it made on her. "I felt love when I was being provided for," she related with emotion, "and I realized it was God who was looking out for me." The power of God's love began to work in the camp, and those traumatized people began to experience hope. By putting the teachings of Jesus to work in their lives, the camp was transformed.

Two years later it was safe to return to their homes in Bundibugyo. With great trepidation they traveled back, not knowing what they would find. Upon returning, they found their homes destroyed, their churches and schools demolished, and almost nothing of their former village intact. It was a time of great sorrow. For two years they had longed to return home, but upon arriving, they found complete devastation. Discouraged and penniless, they again began asking the familiar question, "How can the people from the West help us?"

But Bishop Hannington Bahemuka began to remind them of what God had done in the refugee camp, and he encouraged his people to begin asking a different question. Instead of looking to others for assistance, Hannington told them to ask, "How soon can we rise to the challenge of funding not only our immediate needs, but our future as well?"

He told them he believed God had given them everything they needed locally to rebuild their community. All God needed now was people willing to make themselves available to God. Hannington asked mechanics, builders, and business people to use their gifts to rebuild the community. One by one, person by person, the idea caught on. They began rebuilding their churches and schools and constructing a home for the orphans. People came forward, even in deep poverty, and contributed what they had.

One widow in the church was not only old and extremely poor, but crippled as well. As they were trying to gather materials and funds to build the church, this widow didn't want to be left out. All she possessed was one chicken, so that is what she gave. Word of her sacrificial gift got out, and the story inspired others to share. Today this woman worships in the small brick church that she helped build.

These experiences gave this church a picture of how God intends the church to work. Giving not only provided the needed funds to rebuild, it also blessed the givers and encouraged a spirit of community.

Children also learned lessons through this rebuilding process that will bless Bundibugyo for many generations. They learned that God has given them the resources they need to live and provide for themselves.

Today this same spirit of generosity continues in Bundibugyo. "We once gave out of a sense of duty," says a local church member, "but now we are willing and count it a joy in our hearts." They have seen firsthand how God can use the little they have to transform their community.

The people in Bundibugyo are not interested in foreign aid. Even though life there can be difficult, the joy of providing for themselves has replaced a welfare mentality. As they began using what God had given them, they began to prosper, and a cycle of sustainability began. Today, Bishop Hannington has something he would like to tell other parts of the world. "This message," he said, "can work in every situation and in every country." [1]

Indigenous Sustainability

We all love stories like this. It excites us to see indigenous vision taking root and local people taking responsibility for their own lives. In this chapter we want to look at the importance of sustainability and ways it can be encouraged and fostered. We need to remember as well that the same principles which apply to achieving sustainability in foreign countries are applicable in our local congregations. Hannington Bahemuka learned that transformation was possible in a refugee camp. If sustainability is possible in Uganda, it is also possible for every brother in your congregation who possesses a sound mind and body.

In our world of environmental concerns, sustainability can mean many things. As we use the term here, we are primarily addressing economic sustainability—the ability of an individual, family, or community to provide for their own material needs using their God-given abilities and resources. Earlier we addressed identifying need and noted that the antidote for ongoing need is opportunity. But the opportunity we provide must help them focus on their own resources and abilities, or we will compound the problem.

For example, suppose a man has land but doesn't have tools to farm it. Our first reaction to this scenario is to provide relief by giving him the tools he needs. Sometimes this can provide short-term help. But giving him what he needs rarely moves him closer to long-term sustainability. Rather, what if you could teach him how to save for that tool? This will take longer, but once he understands and embraces this concept, he has the ability to become sustainable. When the tool wears out, this man knows what to do, and he no longer needs you. That is sustainability. Sometimes our impatience and instinctive reactions, both locally and away from home, cause us to become part of the problem instead of the solution.

Steve Saint, the son of martyred missionary Nate Saint, once said, "Financial help that does not develop sustainable, local, financial self-sufficiency is much more likely to produce poverty than it is to meet real needs. Until we realize that we can't overcome poverty with hand-outs, we will never be of much help."[2]

When we address chronic need, our goal must be greater than just making sure we supply relief. The criterion for helping chronic need is whether it actually moves the recipient toward sustainability. With relief, you address symptoms. You give a person food, and that relieves the symptom.

But when attempting to bring opportunity, the goal is to alter established patterns of life. And as all of us who have tried to break a habit know, this will take time. So how do we provide opportunity? And more important, how can we provide opportunity in a way that eventually changes a man's mindset to where he takes responsibility for his own problems? Let's look at three important basic principles in moving a man toward sustainability.

Do No Harm

Picture for a moment one of the poor Israelite families in the Old Testament. Let's suppose the husband of this family was just a little lazy. He didn't get his crops planted quite when he should have, had trouble keeping the weeds out, and for some reason never had enough to provide for his family. He would have been known as poor in Israel, and as we have categorized poverty, his need would have been chronic. God had told Israel how to take care of this kind of poverty: leave the corners of your field, go over your grapes and olives only once, and occasionally leave some of the harvest in the field if you happen to forget it. So when harvest came and this man didn't have much for his family, there was a way for him to survive.

Now visualize harvest time for a moment. This man doesn't have enough. While others fill their barns and pantries, this man faces the prospect of a hungry family in the coming winter. The symptom is a lack of food. But what is the man's real underlying need? He needs to learn the importance of diligence and hard work, and that he has the needed resources to provide for his family.

But suppose his neighbor sees his poverty and begins to provide food each month. What will happen? It is very simple. The poor man will feel no need to go out and harvest the grain, grapes, and olives that the Lord commanded the Israelite farmers to provide for this situation. By providing relief, this neighbor circumvents the poor man's actual need.

Even though he is trying to help, his relief causes long-term harm to this man and his family. When attempting to move the chronically poor from where they are to where they need to be, first make sure your "help" will not actually harm them.

> *To reverse the downward spiral so prevalent in poverty, teaching must be part of our solution.*

Teach Them

Many people grow up with poor role models and very little teaching. To reverse the downward spiral so prevalent in poverty, teaching must be part of our solution. There is a great need in our churches, as well as in developing countries, for teachers. This can be a good fit for older believers who are at a place in life where they have extra time. I have noticed, however, that people in materially poor countries who ask for help rarely believe that business instruction is their primary need. However, after they have received business teaching for a year, they will almost always say the teaching has helped even more than the loan they received. Having good, methodical teaching over an extended period of time is important. Don't expect to take a man who has developed an improper mindset over twenty years and transform his understanding at a two-day seminar. Teaching takes time.

Show Them

Programs that demonstrate sustainability and show how to achieve it are essential. This can take place in a variety of ways. Teaching is important, but you may also need to sit down periodically with a struggling brother in your congregation and *show* him how to set up a budget or keep household records. He may need to meet with a mentor who has traveled down a similar path and has learned from the experience. But again, the goal is to move the person to a place where he no longer needs assistance.

In developing countries, some organizations go out and work with farmers, showing them better techniques and ways of doing things. This is valuable and more effective than teaching alone. But changing long-held farming practices isn't easy. I remember talking to a man several years ago who had poured years into teaching better farming techniques in a small impoverished community. He tried to teach them the importance of fertilizing and showed them how they could take manure from their animals and fertilize their corn. The local people all laughed. Imagine putting donkey manure in the corn field where you were producing food! What a ridiculous idea!

So this man set up an experimental plot. He let them plant some rows of corn right beside his. His corn was fertilized with manure, while theirs was not. Of course, at harvest the difference was obvious. His corn was taller and produced much more than theirs. He felt sure this would convince them. But they initially concluded that he must have sneaked in some special kind of seed. They still didn't believe manure would help. But over a period of several years their farming practices slowly began to change and their lives were improved. This takes much patience. When people are living on the edge and barely surviving, it is hard to convince them to try new techniques. Their current practices produce some food, so why should they take the risk of changing?

You cannot breeze into a community, hold a seminar showing better techniques, and instantly move their community into prosperity. Until you form strong relationships with them, they will find it difficult to trust you enough to take the required risk.

Conclusion

There are several reasons why Hannington Bahemuka successfully moved his people to sustainability in Uganda. The first is that they were his own people. His people trusted him, and one of the most difficult hurdles in developing sustainability is getting local buy-in. But once you have men like Hannington who believe sustainability is possible and who are willing to encourage their people to pursue it, then most of the battle is won. Another reason this community was successful is because someone cared enough to come from a developed country and provide the teaching. They didn't bring in material gifts. If they had, the outcome would have been much different. But they came with a clear message: Ugandans, like all other people on earth, have God-given abilities and resources to sustain themselves. But until we believe this truth ourselves, we will have trouble moving others toward long-term sustainability.

The Search for Sustainability

It was 1976, and the country of Bangladesh was suffering yet another famine. Just five years earlier, the country had won its fight for independence, but the war had taken a heavy toll. Three million Bangladeshis had lost their lives, and millions more had become victims of terrible atrocities committed by the Pakistani army. The economy was shattered, and now with a famine underway, the situation looked desperate.

During this time, Professor Muhammad Yunus, a Bangladeshi economist from Chittagong University, began taking his students on field trips to the poorer areas of Bangladesh. He was looking for ways to help the local farmers become more productive, and he also wanted to show these privileged university students what life was like for the extremely poor. During one of these field trips, Professor Yunus made a discovery that would affect millions of people's lives in many poor countries.

Yunus stopped in the small village of Jobra, and walking up to a little thatched-roof house, he introduced himself and began to interview the lady who lived there. Sufiya Begum had three children and was twenty-one years old. Squatting on the dirt floor in front of the house, she was quickly weaving strands of bamboo together to make a cane stool as they talked. The stool was half finished when Yunus appeared and began asking her about her little business. He was shocked at what he discovered.

Sufiya needed supplies every day to make these small stools, and the bamboo for each stool cost twenty-two cents. But since she didn't have this much money, she had an arrangement with the *paikars,* or middlemen. Since banks are not interested in working with the extremely poor, these men gave her the bamboo on credit, with the agreement that she would bring a finished stool back at the end of each day. After Sufiya had paid a fee for borrowing the bamboo for the day, she had only two cents left over for her day of labor. Yunus couldn't believe what was happening. These middlemen were keeping women like Sufiya trapped in conditions of near slavery. Had she had the capital to purchase her own bamboo, Sufiya could have made much more and helped her family rise out of this miserable poverty. But because she didn't have twenty-two cents of operating capital, she was forced to work hard all day for just two cents! Yunus said later, "I was angry, angry at myself, angry at my economics department and the thousands of intelligent professors who had not tried to address this problem and solve it."[1]

Professor Yunus went home that night disturbed. The absurdity of the situation wouldn't go away. He had seen poverty all his life but had never known anyone condemned to a life of hand-to-mouth survival merely for the lack of twenty-two cents. Yunus returned to the village to do additional research, and during the next week he discovered forty-two women in that little village suffering under the same bondage. So Yunus took twenty-seven dollars from his pocket, loaned a little to each woman, and told them to buy their own bamboo and pay him back with the profits when they could. Of course there were naysayers, but to the surprise of everyone watching his little experiment, all the women repaid their loans.

From this first trial, Grameen Bank was eventually formed for the express purpose of lending to the poor. Millions have benefited from Professor Yunus' experiment. Since that time many organizations have experimented with various lending models, and in this chapter we want to look at some lessons learned during this process.

As we think about the search for sustainability in people's lives, one thing needs to be clearly understood—there is no silver bullet. There is no single foolproof method of dealing with poverty. Multigenerational poverty, whether at home or abroad, has many underlying causes.

Planners and Searchers

In his book, *The White Man's Burden*,[2] William Easterly addresses the difference between people he calls "The Planners" and "The Searchers." A Planner, Easterly says, believes outsiders impose solutions. Planners are foreigners who don't feel the need to ask many questions. They provide broad, sweeping programs that usually cost lots of money and are marketed as the final solution to the problem. Planners are not usually interested in going back years later and analyzing whether or not their solution worked. They are on to the next problem, raising funds and planning a solution.

But Searchers are different. A Searcher hopes to find solutions by trial and error. He knows one solution will not fit every situation. A Searcher also understands he will need some input from the local people to succeed. Easterly also concluded that Searchers have much better results. "The Planners," Easterly says, "have the rhetorical advantage of promising great things: the end of poverty." But the Searchers are the ones who actually make a difference in people's lives and move them, in a variety of ways, out of poverty and on to sustainability. They understand that the causes of poverty are multifaceted, and they will need to employ different tools in different settings. So let's look at a couple of these tools in use today.

Microcredit

Microcredit, first made popular by Muhammad Yunus, has evolved over the years. The basic principle is that a small amount of money is loaned to a poor person to help him start or expand a small business. The goal is to help the poor use their abilities and resources more effectively. This is similar to the Lord's command to leave the corners of the fields for the poor. For microloans to work, the individual must get out and work, plan, and use the resources God has given him. When combined with teaching, microloans can prove extremely helpful. Through these programs, many families can provide food for their children, pay their own school tuition, and even save for future needs without ongoing foreign aid.

In his book, *Giving Wisely?* Jonathan Martin says:

> A loan is perhaps the best gift I can give to help out those suffering in the Third World. If I give a poor family in Sudan a gift of a hundred dollars, they'll likely run out and buy the food and clothing they've been longing for. In a few days the

hundred dollars will be gone, and there will be no lasting change taking place. If, however, I give a loan to this same family, requiring them to pay it back . . . this would force the family to think about starting a business that could generate more income than the loan itself.[3]

Notice his words: "This would force the family to think . . ." Since our primary goal in dealing with chronic need is not to just change the symptoms but to alter the mindset, we need to find ways to help them think. Microloan programs, when combined with close account-ability and good teaching, have this potential. But it needs to be done carefully. Many times when people try this on their own in impover-ished countries, they do more harm than good. Unless we are willing to walk day by day with the person and provide close accountability, the results will most likely disappoint us.

But as Martin says, these programs do force a person to look closely at his business and make sure it actually produces a profit. When you give a person tools, supplies, or money to purchase inventory as a gift, there is no reason for him to analyze the viability of his business. He can rightly assume that if things don't work out, you or someone else will come with another gift to get things going again.

There are exceptions. Organizations can point to a few examples where a gift was given, the man started a business, and today his business is sustainable. But it is rare for gifts to create long-term sustainability.

But while many have received tremendous help though microcredit, the system has some weaknesses as well. In some countries, microloans alone have not always proven to work well with the extremely poor. When people have had no good role models and little incentive to work for several generations, just giving them a loan will not instantly fix their problem. Altering old habits is difficult, and change is slow.

Savings and Credit Associations
Another microfinance model that has become popular in the last few years is the Savings Groups model or Savings & Credit Associations. These programs are structured in various ways, but the basic idea is that poor people meet regularly in groups and pool their savings. Using

this model, they gradually save money, which can then be loaned out to individuals within the group to start businesses or help deal with needs. Poor people, for a variety of reasons, have difficulty in obtaining sums of money large enough to be useful.

In the book, *Portfolios of the Poor,* the authors followed the financial lives of extremely poor people in Bangladesh, India, and South Africa. They asked these families to track, penny by penny, all their financial dealings in an effort to discover how these people manage their money. The results were enlightening. While we assume the poor live simple financial lives, this study revealed that their finances can be amazingly complex. Surviving on two dollars a day isn't easy. But the most difficult part of their struggle isn't that they live on two dollars a day as much as the fact that it doesn't come regularly every day.

We tend to assume the poor don't save. But because their income is so erratic and unpredictable, they have no choice. They must save in some way to survive. Their primary problem, it was discovered, is not that they don't save, but that they save in poor ways. They don't have good places to hold what they are saving. For example, many poor people's savings are invested in animals. If they know school tuition is due in September, they may buy a pig in May. They fatten the pig until September and then sell it to pay tuition. This is a kind of forced saving since the pig will squeal if it isn't fed. And if everything goes right, the plan may work. But what happens if the pig dies? Or what happens to the price of hogs when an entire village tries to sell their pigs in September? There's no tuition money, and no school for their children.

One of the roles of Savings & Credit Associations is to help provide a safe place for savings. Some villages obtain a steel box, put several locks on it, and give the keys to different persons so that several people must be present to open the box. This provides indigenous accountability.

Savings groups have several beautiful benefits. First, they require little outside funding—an important factor. Remember, we are trying to change how they see themselves and their resources. Savings groups can help them understand that God has given them the resources to survive where they are without outside funding. This takes time, but it can happen. Savings groups can also even out the irregularity of income. By having a safe place to deposit cash when it is plentiful and withdraw from when things get tight, a man's financial life becomes more stable and predictable. We tend to forget the blessing of our modern banking system.

As with every model, savings groups have some weaknesses as well. Imagine for a moment that you have twenty people meeting each Saturday morning and depositing two dollars each into the savings group. Within three weeks you have $120 saved, enough for one of them to start a small business. This is wonderful for one of these individuals, but there are nineteen others who also want to start a business, and it will take many months and meetings before all of them can receive a loan from the group.

This is one of the primary weaknesses of savings groups. It takes a long time to see discernible change. But they do produce results. When people finally get a picture of what they can accomplish by working together as a community and slowly saving over time, they begin to see themselves and their resources differently. That, after all, is the goal!

Sustainability Here?

One of the questions repeatedly asked is, "All this is happening in other countries, but what about sustainability here in America? Are there any programs available here to help people provide for themselves?"

As we have mentioned several times, the basic principles required for sustainability work in any culture. Although the dollar amounts people work with will be different in a developed country, the underlying principles remain the same. In 1986, Grameen Bank began experimenting with microfinance in the United States. At first many were skeptical that this model could be effective in the inner cities of America, but their program has proved successful so far, and other organizations are using this model as well. All they do is provide capital and opportunity to those who have had little of either.

Conclusion

Many attempts are being made to provide sustainable solutions to the poor, and the need remains tremendous. While Professor Yunus worked primarily with commerce and sustainable businesses, others focus on agriculture and try to provide better erosion control and more productive varieties of produce. Others focus on education, and still others on promoting saving groups. But in any of these areas, we must remember some basic truths if we want to provide long-term sustainable solutions.

1. **Sustainability takes time.** Our culture has taught us to expect instant results, and we become impatient when change doesn't come quickly. Harvest does not come immediately after planting. Be cautious about giving to any person or organization that promises instant sustainability.

2. **Never provide what the individual can provide for himself.** I mentioned this before, but it needs to be implanted in our minds. Many people need opportunity. But when we go beyond and donate resources the people already have, we ultimately harm the very ones we are trying to help.

3. **Restoration, not just relief, is the goal.** When we work with people in need, our goal is not just to relieve. It is to work with God in changing their current world view to where God wants it to be—to help them establish a correct view of God, of their environment, and of themselves as children of God. Trying to change symptoms while ignoring the underlying mindset that produced them will ultimately create dependency. Short-term answers to long-term problems create long-lasting dependency.

> *Short-term answers to long-term problems create long-lasting dependency.*

THE SEARCH FOR SUSTAINABILITY

197

Let Them Be Children of God

W hen those four lepers on the affluent side of the wall in Samaria suddenly realized their great responsibility to those starving on the other side of the wall, they knew they had to share. They saw critical need, and the solution was obvious—open the gate and let the abundance from one side flow to meet the needs on the other side. Those lepers had the responsibility and the opportunity to begin the transfer of aid to the needy.

Recently I met a man whose job had been similar to the mission of these lepers. John's job was to travel to extremely poor countries, analyze requests, and then travel back to America to raise funds to meet those needs. John had helped with this for several years, raising money for church-building projects, various programs, and humanitarian aid. So back and forth John went, from meetings with the extremely poor to meetings with the very affluent. As he gave presentations to the affluent, John tried to convey the deep need he saw among the poor, hoping wealthy donors would give generously and meet the need.

But one day as John traveled back to America with yet more needs to present, something suddenly occurred to him. He realized it was impossible to raise enough money to provide for all the needs he had just encountered. He looked over the list of churches where he was to speak, and he knew it just wouldn't happen. So what was he to do?

For the first time, John told me, he began to back up and analyze supply and demand. He concluded that either he would need to squeeze more from wealthy donors, or the people asking for help would need to find other ways to meet their own needs. John began to think back over his work of the last few years and realized there was something else that troubled him. He had helped transfer a great deal of aid to many churches, but his efforts didn't seem to move them in the direction of sustainability. In fact, some of those who had received the most seemed to be needier than ever.

John ultimately concluded that this paternalistic approach was teaching them to become children of American churches rather than children of God. Instead of teaching them to be industrious, he was encouraging laziness and teaching them to look to others for aid. That day profoundly affected John's life, and today he operates a ministry that goes into extremely poor countries, teaching them how to rely totally on local resources.

Keep in mind that John is not working with critical need. The focus of his ministry is in poor countries that have struggled for years, such as Kenya, Bangladesh, and Guatemala. Even though these countries have poverty, they also have their own natural resources. John's focus has shifted from searching for resources in developed countries to finding solutions and resources within the needy communities themselves.

John saw the need for sustainability and began teaching the importance of it. This shift in focus wasn't easy for him, but today John can point to many totally sustainable churches because of that instruction. They are constructing their own buildings, helping the handicapped among them, and learning to save for future church planting.

Christians in developed countries receive much teaching on the importance of giving. We hear ministers contrasting the Sea of Galilee to the Dead Sea. Both have water pouring into them, but the one with nothing flowing out is known as the Dead Sea. Christians, we are told, are the same. God continues to pour blessing into our lives, but unless that blessing flows on to others, we will lack spiritual life and vitality. Since there is great blessing in giving, shouldn't the poor be given the opportunity as well?

Does Everyone Need to Give?

Earlier we looked at the example set by the church in Mizoram, India, where they use a simple program known as *Buhfai Tham*, or *A Handful of Rice*. This program's basic premise is that every believer should be giving in some way. If giving is such a blessing and is so essential to a believer's spiritual life in developed countries, shouldn't believers in poorer settings contribute something as well? Or are some people so poor that God does not expect them to give? Let's look at a few examples in Scripture about giving among the poor.

After Elijah had predicted a terrible drought on the country of Israel, God sent him to a poor widow in Zarephath. From our perspective this was about the worst place a man could go to find sustenance. Not only was she a widow, but she already had a son to support. Furthermore, she was down to her last meal when Elijah arrived.[a] Yet God sent Elijah there to ask this woman to support him. Why did God require this woman to give? Why didn't He send Elijah to one of the wealthy people in the country?

We think differently than God. While we look for supply to meet the demand, God looks for faith. He found it in this extremely poor widow. She believed in the power of God to provide, gave all she had, and was blessed by God in a way she could never have anticipated.

What about the widow who willingly gave her last two mites?[b] Again, this account flies in the face of common sense. Why not let that poor woman keep her pittance and ask one of the wealthy men in the city to chip in a little more? But God used this widow to display His heart

> *While we look for supply to meet the demand, God looks for faith.*

regarding the importance of sacrificial giving, and the message is clear: God expects the poor to give.

As you look back over the teachings in the Bible, all the way from Genesis to Revelation, can you think of anyone who was so poor that God exempted him from giving? Can you think of even one example? God loves to exhibit His ability to provide when people are out of resources, and I suspect the widow who threw all her living into the temple treasury found her life blessed in ways she could never have imagined. I don't think she went back home only to die within a few

---

[a] 1 Kings 17:8-16

[b] Luke 21:1-4

days because she gave.

God loves to see His children give cheerfully, and He loves to bless the man who puts his trust in Him. We do a great disservice to less privileged believers when we remove their incentive to share and deny them the privilege of giving.

Why Should I Give?

Warren Buffet is known as one of the richest men in the world. Through the years he has made many shrewd financial moves and has accumulated a tremendous amount of earthly wealth. In 2012, *Forbes Magazine* estimated Buffet's wealth at approximately $46 billion.[1]

Now let's suppose Warren Buffet suddenly became a believer and wanted to become a member of your church. And let's assume his assets were earning 5 percent (a return that in real life would be disappointingly low to him), and he was convicted of his need to give 10 percent of his yearly increase in net worth to the Lord. Let's also suppose he was so grateful to the wonderful people in your congregation who led him to the Lord that he wanted to funnel all his giving through your church.

So Warren does the math, comes to church next Sunday, and dumps around $4.5 million into the church treasury. Not only that, but it suddenly dawns on the congregation that another $4.5 million will come next Sunday, and the one after that, and the one after that.

Now let's imagine your family has been on a tight budget, trying to give as much as possible to the work of the Lord. Let's say you had tightened down the screws and were able to give $104.35 each week. What would happen when Brother Warren starts dropping $4.5 million into the treasury every week? How long would you keep giving your paltry little offering? Can you imagine how insignificant it would appear? And what about next fall when it is announced the church needs a new roof? How much would your family sacrifice, knowing Brother Warren, sitting on the pew behind you, gives enough to replace the entire church building every day?

If you are normal, admitting Warren Buffett into your church would greatly affect your giving. You would probably have a different view of giving, over time, and the joy and blessing you presently experience by sharing would be lost.

This is the situation we place upon believers in many foreign countries when we jump into their communities with almost endless resources. We become Brother Warren. And unless we are extremely careful, we can destroy the blessing and joy of sacrificial giving that God intended His children to enjoy. It is so easy for us to rob the poor of this blessing.

A widow once came to a church meeting in Brighton, England, and at the conclusion of the meeting she presented the pastor with a gold sovereign. The pastor, knowing her poverty, refused to accept the large coin. He began to tell this woman she had no business giving this much, but he paused as he noticed her great agitation.

"Oh sir," she said, "I have often given pieces of copper to the Lord. Two or three times I have had the joy to give Him pieces of silver. But it has been the grand desire of my life to give Him a piece of gold before I die. For a long time I have been putting by all that I was able in order to make this sum. Take it, I pray you, for the cause!"[2] So often we forget the desperate need every believer has, regardless of his comparative worth, to give.

Recently a brother shared a similar experience. He was traveling in the States near a large city and needed to briefly pull off the road to use his phone. As he was parked there, he noticed a homeless lady at a nearby intersection asking for donations from those who stopped.

A few minutes later he heard a tapping on his window, and looking up, he saw this woman just outside his car. The brother lowered his window a little and listened to the familiar story of poor choices, bad relationships, and financial need. Evening was approaching, and having no place to sleep, she asked for money to get a room for the night. This brother wasn't sure what to do. Would she really use the money for that? Would he actually help her by giving her cash? But moved by the tears and the story, he gave her the money she requested, and she went back to her place at the intersection.

A few minutes later, still talking on his phone, this brother again heard a tapping on the glass. The woman was there again, but this time, instead of asking, she had something she wanted to share with him. Someone had given this woman an apple and a small bag of cashews. In thankfulness for the larger gift she had received from this brother, she wanted to give something in return. He tried to object, but ultimately relented when it was obvious she needed to give something back. Sometimes it is easier to give than to receive—especially from a homeless woman. But we must remember that God created us all with an inborn need to give. When we deny the poor this privilege, we keep them from being everything God intended.

Conclusion

As you help others, give them the opportunity to learn responsibility. Let them experience the joy of paying for services they receive from others. Allow them the pleasure of thinking, planning, and charting their own course to sustainability. Let them save and pay for the tools, products, and supplies required to expand their businesses. Don't rob them of that feeling of accomplishment which comes from providing for their own. And don't forget to let them give!

We have looked at the importance of giving. It is vital to our Christian life for blessings to flow from us. It is an integral part of becoming conformed to the image of Jesus Christ. Our Father is continually pouring blessing into our lives, and it is imperative that blessings flow from us—from *all* of us, even the materially poor!

PART
SIX

*Using the
Resources God
Has Given Us*

Good Literature

Throughout this book I have emphasized the need for teaching in our pursuit of sustainability. Wrong concepts have been passed down through generations. Without corrective teaching, developing countries will continue to make the same mistakes year after year. But when you try to find good teaching material to use in this effort, the shortage is astounding! Billions of dollars have been spent to feed, clothe, and house the poor. Yet in contrast, much less emphasis is being given to good literature to help them learn better methods.

There is a great hunger for teaching in developing countries, and when good literature is provided, it is valued highly. Recently I attended a meeting in Ghana where people who had started small businesses through a lending program gathered to receive ongoing training. They had all received a teaching manual when they entered the program, but as they assembled, I initially did not see any manuals.

However, as they took their seats, they began unwrapping small bundles they had carried with them, and inside were their manuals. To keep them clean, they had wrapped them in used plastic bags. For many of them, their instructor informed me, this was the only literature in their home.

Our world is so different. My shelf holds books I haven't opened in years, and I would never miss some of them if they disappeared. But for these small business owners, there is so much they want to learn, and good teaching material is essential to their success. Many of them were never taught before how to keep good records, save for inventory replacement, or put a business plan together.

Value of the Written Word
But the disparity between the developed and underdeveloped worlds

involves more than just good business teaching. Of even greater importance is the need for Bibles and good spiritual teaching. On our side of the wall are plenty of Bibles and Christian literature, but on the other side millions are starving for the Word of God and Scriptural teaching, This seems strange to us who have grown up surrounded by an abundance of Bibles. We not only have access to Bibles, but we can choose which version we prefer. We can decide if we want large print, small print, or the words of Jesus in red letters, and we can select from a large assortment of colored bindings. In the last few years, many are listening to audio Bibles, and once again there is a vast array of options. The listener can select the reader's voice, decide whether or not to play background music, and even choose to hear the sound of the angry mob when listening to the account of the crucifixion.

But on the other side of the wall the situation is entirely different. Millions still long for the day when they can hold their first Bible or find sound Christian literature for themselves and their families.

Sound preaching is wonderful, but the printed page has the ability to continue to teach after the instructor moves. Puritan writer Thomas Brooks once said, "Books may preach when the author cannot; when the author may not; when the author dares not; yes, and which is more, when the author is not."

> *Millions still long for the day when they can hold their first Bible.*

Even ungodly men have recognized the power of the written page. When Lenin took over Russia, he said, "The people will never believe or understand communism unless they are indoctrinated with communism by the printed page." Lenin understood the power of the printed page and put forth a great deal of effort to promote literacy. He wanted every man, woman, and child to read his doctrine.

Connecting the Gift to the Giver

Whether engaged in a project aiming for sustainability or while providing relief after a disaster, Christian literature has the ability to connect our efforts to God, and our gift to the Ultimate Giver.

Recently I was talking with a Christian brother who has helped in various relief efforts following natural catastrophes. He spoke of the increased openness in countries immediately after a disaster, and the great opportunity there is for distributing literature.

"The country of Japan," he told me, "has had Bibles available for many years. But the tremendous earthquake in 2011 got their attention and caused many to stop and reconsider their lives."

He went on to describe how people who had been taught evolution, reincarnation, and self-sufficiency suddenly came face to face with their own vulnerability. When the ground began to shake under them, it forced them to reevaluate their beliefs. Consequently, there was a great openness to literature among the Japanese.

Other disasters in Myanmar, Pakistan, and Haiti have provided similar opportunities. Catastrophes in Bangladesh have opened many doors that were previously locked. They gave an opening for Christians to go in, work with their hands, develop relationships, and demonstrate what the Gospel looks like in everyday life. Many people in these countries have been taught that Christians are aggressive warmongers. Seeing unselfish people reach out to them in a time of need has a way of softening hearts. It also provides an opportunity to distribute Bibles and Christian literature, and sometimes God uses this material to impact lives in astounding ways.

One Bible in a Basement

Mikhailo was raised in Ukraine in the 1970s. Following his graduation from an Orthodox seminary, Mikhailo became a professor and trained new priests.

Mikhailo seemed to be at the peak of his career, and he enjoyed his life as a professor. The pay was good, and he could focus on encouraging other young men to seek after God. But one day one of his students asked a question that started Mikhailo on a search with long-lasting implications.

"Why," the student asked, "do the Orthodox and Catholic churches baptize infants, while other Christian churches baptize adults?"

This seemed like a simple question, but as Mikhailo began to read

THE OTHER SIDE OF THE WALL

and study, it dawned on him that infant baptism was based solely on the doctrines and traditions of his church. He struggled with this. Why didn't his reference books contain quotes from the Bible itself? And as Mikhailo pondered, doubts began to swirl in his mind. Was the Orthodox teaching correct? Why did other professing Christians practice baptism differently? What was truth?

One day, rummaging around in the basement of the monastery where they kept discarded and unnecessary items, he found the book that would change his life. It was a Bible.

A Bible?

As I listened to Mikhailo tell his story, I didn't grasp the significance of finding a Bible. Surely a seminary professor with years of training was well versed in the Bible. But no, Mikhailo told me, until that day he had never actually held a Bible in his hand. The only Scriptures he had read were portions carefully selected by church authorities and printed in the Orthodox doctrinal material he had studied. No one at his level, not even a priest or seminary professor, was allowed to read the Bible for himself.

This Bible had been given to another seminary student by a Mennonite missionary, disposed of by the fearful student in the basement, and had now found its way to Mikhailo. He opened it and began to read, but fearful of being caught, he abandoned the book and headed back up the stairs.

Three days passed. But during those days his mind continued to churn with questions. Finally, driven by a desire for truth, Mikhailo went back to the basement and began secretly reading this Bible for himself. Slowly he began to comprehend that what he had been taught and was teaching was wrong. Mikhailo began to voice his observations to a few others and was warned to be quiet. But how can a man stay quiet when his heart is full of the truth of God's Word?

Finally his exasperated superiors gave him an isolated position far from the seminary, but this simply gave Mikhailo more unsupervised time to examine the Scriptures. For six months he read, learned, and became more convicted of God's calling. During this time he lost his fear of man, and it became clear he needed to make a clean break with the Orthodox Church.

That wasn't an easy choice. For twenty-two years Mikhailo had devoted his life entirely to the church. His parents had died, and now Mikhailo had no possessions, no income to sustain him, and no place to live. But Mikhailo trusted the Lord, and since the day he walked away from the Orthodox Church, his life has changed completely. A man like this is a great threat to the established church, and attempts have been made on his life.

But imagine the blessing Mikhailo is to those who still wander in darkness. Through this converted priest, others are coming to believe in the Lord Jesus. Light is shining out from a transformed man, and yet, amazingly, this great transformation can be traced back to someone caring enough to share a Bible.

Conclusion

Those of us in the developed world listen to accounts like Mikhailo's and marvel at how God completely transformed his life. Knowing that this transformation can be traced back to someone caring enough to share a three-dollar Bible forces me to analyze my use of resources. How many times have I wasted three dollars on some item that has no long-term value? How many more Mikhailos are out there still searching for truth?

Literature alone will not take care of every need or situation. But whether we give Bibles to someone who has never had one, try to move people toward natural sustainability, or encourage someone toward a closer relationship with Jesus Christ, literature is one of the valuable resources God has given us. There is a desperate need for more Christian teaching material and Bibles in our world. Many still wait for the Word of God to be translated into their own language. According to the Wycliffe Bible translators, there are still around 350 million people on the earth right now who do not have a Bible available in their language, and no translation project has even begun for them. Even in many countries where the Bible has been translated, extreme poverty and illiteracy keeps seekers from experiencing the blessing of reading the Word of God for themselves. We have access to Bibles, good teaching material, and Christian literature. They are desperately needed on the other side of the wall.

The Power of the Local Church

Throughout the book of Acts, men were sent out to evangelize. Yet their goal was not only to save people, but also to plant vibrant, self-propagating congregations. There was a focus on organizing, strengthening, and encouraging churches by traveling to visit them and by writing letters of instruction. In fact, a large percentage of the writings in the New Testament are letters to encourage and instruct churches. Church planting was central.

Much of what is termed evangelism today is more individualistic than the picture we get in Acts. One man feels a burden, tries to share that burden and raise financial support, and then goes out to reach as many souls as he can. While all of us should do personal, daily evangelism, I get a deeper, fuller picture in the early church. I see congregations sending people out, not as individuals detached from the body, but as extensions and expressions of the local sending church itself. Sometimes we read of persecution scattering new believers, and as they traveled, they preached the Gospel of Jesus Christ. But other times church planting was an intentional pursuit.

For example, when persecution broke out in Jerusalem, the believers were scattered, preaching as they went.[a] Some of them ended up in Antioch, and through their preaching, more people came to the faith.[b] A new congregation was formed in this heathen city, and just two chapters later we see this new church fasting and praying and sending out Paul and Barnabas.[c] It would seem this fledgling congregation could have used more time to mature and benefit from Paul and Barnabas'

---

[a] Acts 8:1

[b] Acts 11:19-26

[c] Acts 13:3

teaching before sending them out. But remember, their goal wasn't to just encourage, strengthen, and stabilize, but to form churches that could plant other churches as soon as possible.

This wasn't just a few men getting a notion to go somewhere. It was the church, under the Holy Spirit's direction, sending out a part of themselves into unreached pagan communities. They used the vehicle of preaching and church planting. Churches starting new churches with the express intent that these churches would replicate and continue to spread the Gospel.

A Shift in Vision

But looking at church history, we see an obvious shift in vision, and the original church-planting model was neglected. As one author has said, "The history of missions is in the main the history of great personalities and of missionary societies. Only in exceptional cases has it been the church in missions."[1] When you reflect on your knowledge of missions, what do you think of and what do you predominantly read about? Isn't it individual names and great personalities that come to mind?

Now, make no mistake. Many have given their lives to go out and share the Gospel, and much good has been done. There are many first-generation believers around the globe today because someone came to share. There have also been a few examples, like the Moravians, who used a church-planting model. But for the most part, the focus has been on individuals. I admire many who went out by themselves to share the Gospel, and I appreciate what has been accomplished. But I believe God's original intent was for evangelism to be an integral part of the church itself, not just a tacked-on program for only a few.

> *God's original intent was for evangelism to be an integral part of the church itself, not just a tacked-on program for only a few.*

Why Has Church Planting Been Neglected?

This question may have several answers. Some have contended that the change came during the Reformation when some reformers taught that only certain people should reach out to the unsaved. One author says, "Zwingli maintained that mission is the business of specially called apostles, and that the church as such has nothing to do with missions. This same idea carried over later into Pietism and became dominant in much of Western Protestantism."[2] If this author is correct, we are back to our earlier discussion about the root cause of drift in our churches. Perhaps the model was lost due to a fascination with Protestant theology, quick results, and their individualistic approach to evangelism.

But I believe something else has been neglected, and this is Jesus' own teaching on the value of community and brotherhood. John records some of Jesus' final words before He went to the cross, and it is fascinating how much He focused on loving each other.[d] He almost seemed preoccupied with this theme. Repeatedly in the seventeenth chapter of John, Jesus emphasizes the importance of believers loving other believers and then concludes by explaining why this is so important—that the world may also believe and know that God sent Jesus![e] Jesus intended that unity and love within His church testify of His power and presence.

This thought is reiterated in the upper room where Jesus made another powerful declaration: "A new commandment I give unto you, that ye love one another; as I have loved you, that ye also love one another. By this shall all men know that ye are my disciples, if ye have love one to another."[f]

By This Shall All Men Know!

Letting all men know is the goal of evangelism, and Jesus tells how this will occur. He says all people will know when they see how believers love each other. I have wondered many times why we hear so little about these words when we discuss evangelism. Is it possible that part of our difficulty in evangelism, especially in our Western culture, stems from our lack of love and community? Is our primary hindrance something as simple as a lack of people willing to love sacrificially, submit completely, and serve within their local church unconditionally?

[d] John 13-17
[e] John 17:21; 17:23
[f] John 13:34, 35

I have listened to young men pray fervently for the unreached and discuss with great zeal their desire to spread the Gospel. I have enjoyed their enthusiasm as they discuss better methods of dialogue with the lost, effective signage, and how to best distribute tracts. All of these are important and are being used to expand the Kingdom.

But in view of this teaching on the value of a loving community, why does mentioning the need for submission to a local body of believers tend to bring tense silence to these discussions? Somehow we have trouble connecting the submission to authority with evangelism. In their defense, many youth in conservative churches have seen submission promoted only as a means of preservation. And while there is value in preserving Christ-honoring traditions and a healthy Christian culture, these words of Jesus suggest something entirely different. He is saying that a loving brotherhood will loudly proclaim to the surrounding world that Jesus Himself is in their midst.

> *Sacrificial love between believers is the billboard that proclaims the presence of Jesus!*

I feel unqualified to make many bold statements on this topic. But I do believe we should discuss these teachings of Jesus and consider a few questions. Could it be that a local body of believers, in which each member loves and is willing to cheerfully submit to the others in the name of Jesus, is the most powerful method of getting people's attention and turning hearts to the Lord? Can you think of any other organization where people submit to each other in love and sacrificially give of themselves for the good of the others with no visible earthly reward? Willingness to submit to others is extremely rare in our self-centered world. No wonder Jesus said this is how people will know we are His disciples. Sacrificial love between believers is the billboard that proclaims the presence of Jesus!

Perhaps this is why the early church focused on a church-planting model in their evangelistic endeavors. They knew the world needs to see love in action. In my work with a variety of Anabaptist foreign missions, I have observed the effectiveness of this model. I can think of several settings where a local church was organized, problems came, the church worked through the issues with great love, and the influence of that love caused others to stop and ask what made those people love each other like that. Love moves people.

But what about right here in our developed country? What would happen if our churches began using this model to reach out to our communities? What if we could regain a vision for loving, self-sacrificing communities, not only for preservation, but as a method of spreading the Gospel? It is working effectively in developing countries, but could a church-planting model work in our developed countries and communities as well?

I like to imagine congregations who demonstrate both a love for each other and a united concern for the lost. I dream of communities of believers, like torches in a dark night, where love between believers causes a man to pause mid-step to consider what he might be missing. I believe that is God's original design, and He still intends for us to use this model today. Church planting is not just another program, but rather, an overriding vision integrally connected to every other activity and pursuit.

Migrating to Survive Naturally

As many of our forefathers moved to America from Europe in the 1700s and then slowly migrated west in the 1800s, it seems one of their primary goals in migration was survival. They were looking for cheaper farmland and ways to provide for their families. Many during those years struggled to survive, and it took much energy and focus just to put food on the table. As they moved across the country, new churches were planted, and the Gospel spread to new communities. There is nothing wrong with relocating to survive, and I believe God has used migration, like persecution in the early church, to spread the message of the Gospel.

Migrating to Survive Spiritually

But as North America became more developed and survival became less difficult, people began to move between congregations and even geographically for a different reason. Life was easier now, and the motivation wasn't survival, but ideology. Maybe they didn't like the emphasis in one congregation or area and decided to move to another. Or sensing apathy and spiritual indifference, they became concerned about their children, so they moved out and started new congregations. Again, even though the primary motivation wasn't to reach out to others, the Gospel spread and many came to know the Lord because of these new congregations.

Migrating to Spread the Gospel

But I wonder, in light of the words of Jesus and the example of the early church, if it is time to be more purposeful. Are we in a time when more of us should be moving, primarily motivated by the goal of planting churches and spreading the Gospel? I do not claim to have heard a direct voice from God on this topic, but I do believe we should prayerfully consider this thought. Jesus said we are the salt of the earth. But was He picturing large piles of salt in a few locations, or was He envisioning salt spread out to reach more unbelievers?

> *Is it possible that some of our internal problems result from piling up salt and failing to spread out?*

All of us are aware that Satan is turning up the heat on our local congregations. Any church that takes an active stand against the kingdom of darkness will be tried. But some of our problems may also be self-inflicted. Is it possible that some of our internal problems result from piling up salt and failing to spread out? In light of this question, consider some potential benefits to a vibrant church-planting model that encourages spawning new congregations:

- It helps keep the church's focus outward. There are so many needs around us, and when a congregation's energy pours into the lives of those outside the church, we have less energy to expend on examining each other. When our overriding purpose is to expand the Kingdom and promote holiness in the life of each fellow believer, we have less tendency for fault finding and comparing among ourselves.

- Outsiders ask good questions. It is easy to cling to inconsistent opinions and lifestyle choices when there is no one to

THE POWER OF THE LOCAL CHURCH

point them out. But those who have not been raised in our culture can spot these inconsistencies quite quickly, and this can be a great blessing to a congregation. Moving out into new areas will bring more questions.

- I have noticed that children whose parents reach out to the lost usually feel like part of the team. As they grow up learning to pray for their neighbors and being taught to reach out to others in love, it affects their own hearts as well. They learn early to engage in the battle.

- Moving and starting new communities will not be for every family, and some must stay with each planting. But understanding that the purpose is to share and spread helps maintain focus, even for those called to stay. Materialism and continual business expansion distract us less as we purposely develop a vision for church planting.

I believe we are in a time when we should closely consider our overall vision. Our primary goal is not to evangelize or plant churches. The primary goal must always be to follow Christ. But following in His steps *will* affect our burden for others and how we reach out.

While I was visiting a small church in a developing country, one of the members who had initially moved to that area shared some thoughts on congregation size that have stuck with me. He said when their family moved, they came with just one other family. This forced them to get acquainted with their neighbors, and in that way their church grew. Today they have five churches in that area.

As I consider this, I realize more how much energy is spent internally as a congregation grows. Leaders need to focus more on internal needs, lessening their energy to reach out to others. But I wonder what would happen if our congregations were smaller and kept spreading to new areas. Would we have more contact with seekers and more opportunity to demonstrate a vibrant church life that shows the love of Christ collectively?

Conclusion

We are living in the last days. It seems Satan is pulling out every stop and using every trick to distract and confuse people. There is a push to chase every pleasure, possession, and pursuit that the flesh longs for. It is a self-focused, self-centered, and self-indulgent age. And yet, as people chase down all these egocentric roads, they are obviously miserable. Even though almost every conceivable electronic gadget, pleasurable pursuit, and recreational diversion is available, something is missing. I see evidence of this on faces in airports and in shopping centers, and even on the faces of the rich and famous. People are not finding what they are seeking.

But against this dark, depressing, and self-centered backdrop, God calls the church in our day to shine. He calls us to demonstrate something radically different, and I believe He intends it to be done through the local church.

Imagine for a moment a church where love is so strong among its members that nobody could divide them. A church, like the early church, that is so focused on building the Kingdom, its people are willing to put their entire lives, even their money and possessions, on the table. A congregation where its members so badly want to submit to each other that they never think of brotherhood agreements as restrictions.

As you consider reaching out to others in these last days, think about the impact a loving, selfless, and Kingdom-focused congregation could have on our culture. It seems every church out there is proclaiming that they have an inside edge on truth and that their doctrine is superior in some way. Yet few seekers are persuaded by this doctrinal wrangling. It is time the church again embraces the simple truth contained in these words of Jesus: "By this shall all men know that ye are my disciples, if ye have love one to another."[g]

---

[g] John 13.35

Stewarding Our Material Resources

I n the central part of the state of Washington is a small valley called the Kittitas Valley. It is a beautiful farming community, and one of its distinguishing features is its view of Mount Stuart. On a clear day, this mountain with its sharp, snowcapped peak stands out sharply against a beautiful blue sky, and it has found itself in many camera viewfinders. In fact, the view of the mountain is so prominent that many homes in the area have been built at odd angles to the passing road, just to enable the occupants to get a better view of Mount Stuart.

For thirteen years our family lived on the south slope of the Kittitas Valley, and our home was one of those built to face Mount Stuart. Even though the mountain was forty miles away, on a clear day its massive slopes and jagged peak seemed to be just outside the front window.

I enjoy mornings, and one of my favorite memories is of sitting in my chair (which also faced Mount Stuart) sipping coffee and watching the early morning sunlight hit the peak of the mountain. The bottom of the snow-covered mountain would still be dark, and it was an awesome sight to watch those first rays glisten off the peak. It was a beautiful way to begin a day.

But in spite of the sheer beauty of the sight, there was one small problem. Directly between our house and Mount Stuart was a telephone pole. As I sat in my chair and gazed at the mountain, this telephone pole always partially obstructed my view.

We talked at different times

about how nice it would be to move the telephone pole. "Life would be perfect," we would joke, "if we didn't have to look at that pole."

One day a utility crew was working in front of our house, and I asked the men about this offending pole. I told the foreman about our dilemma and how we wished the pole would go away. The foreman was understanding and said it wouldn't be difficult to move it. They could run the wire underground for a distance, and then the pole would no longer obstruct our view.

I had never seriously considered moving the pole, but I asked him how much this would cost. The foreman did a little figuring and said it would be about seven thousand dollars. This seemed expensive just to improve our view, but I went back to the house and relayed this discussion to my family. All of us got a good laugh out of it but really didn't give it any more thought.

But occasionally, as we sat with visitors on our front porch, sipping iced tea and looking out across the beautiful valley at Mount Stuart, I would retell the story of the $7,000 pole. Our guests would look at the offending pole, and as they heard the cost to move it, their varied responses interested me. Some felt like spending seven thousand dollars to move a pole sounded extravagant, but others said they would move it if they lived there. One pointed out that if we ever sold the property, we might get our money back. Others said it would be worth the money just to have a perfect view. But some disagreed. They said the resale argument can be used to justify just about anything we want, and many unnecessary home improvements are rationalized by claiming we are improving the resale value.

Reference Points

So how do we decide issues like this? As stewards of God's resources, is it acceptable to move the pole? How you answer this question will be determined largely by what you use as a reference point.

Suppose you lived there along the south slope of the Kittitas Valley. Imagine your house was paid off, you are giving 10 percent of your income to the Kingdom, and you have $7,000 in the bank. Would it be acceptable as a steward to move the pole? Does no debt and enough cash in the bank mean it would be acceptable?

Or change the scenario. Imagine the same situation, but instead of $7,000 you have $100,000 in the bank. Now would it be okay to move the pole? Does more available money change the equation? How do we determine when it is acceptable to move the telephone pole?

There are many variables, and each of us might draw the line in a slightly different spot. Let's look briefly at a few potential reference points we might use in considering whether or not to move the pole.

- **Ownership:** Establishing ownership is essential. If we conclude that the money we have in the bank is our own and solely for our enjoyment, then the answer is obvious—move the pole and enjoy the view. But if we examine these questions from a Biblical or stewardship point of view, we may come to a different conclusion. If God owns the resources we have at our disposal, then things aren't quite so simple, and it would be only logical to consult Him. Is moving the pole really where God wants us to use His resources? This simple concept of ownership is foundational as a reference point and will impact our decisions.

- **Disparity:** Another point of reference is the inequality in our world. Go back for a moment to those lepers who stumbled across all that food and wealth just outside the city of Samaria. Why did they conclude they were not doing well? Was it because they didn't have a right to the abundance that lay before them? No, God had miraculously provided it, and they could have argued they had every right to help themselves. But their consciences began to churn. They remembered those just over the wall who were starving, and something didn't seem right. Disparity should also be a reference point in our decision about whether or not to move the telephone pole. Is it right to improve my view when I know there are many in great need?

- **Obligation or opportunity?** Do you see need in the lives of others as an obligation or an opportunity? As you walk through a normal day, do you find yourself primarily looking for ways to improve and enhance your personal enjoyment, or do you look for ways to develop the natural and spiritual lives of others? I don't believe the Lord intends for us to live depressed, discouraged lives. Neither do I feel He expects us to give no thought to personal comfort. I think Jesus ate when He was hungry and slept when He was tired without feeling guilty for time wasted. But He did leave us a clear example, a reference point, of primarily focusing on others even at the expense of personal comfort.[a] How we see needs in the lives of others will impact whether or not we move the pole.

- **Comparing ourselves with others:** Imagine that everyone else in your congregation lived along the same road facing Mount Stuart, and they had all moved the obstructing poles in front of their homes. Would this impact your decision? I wish I could say this would have no bearing on my decision. But as I look back at decisions I have made, I think it would. Paul told the church of Corinth not to measure themselves by themselves and compare themselves among themselves. Paul says don't do it, and yet we do. Instead of prayerfully considering what God has in mind, I would probably look up and down the road to see what my brothers and sisters are doing. Somehow a little wastefulness with our Lord's goods doesn't seem too bad as long as others are engaged in it as well.

Conclusion

I have used this story numerous times in financial seminars and have concluded that we all have "telephone poles" in our lives. Our lives would be a little nicer if certain things would just go away. They are little difficulties that keep life from being just the way we would like, and with a little money we could move them out of the way. So we wrestle with these issues and wonder how much of God's resources we should use to move the telephone poles in our lives.

I believe God intends that we each wrestle with these telephone poles

---

[a] Philippians 2:6-8; 2 Corinthians 8:9

and exercise love toward our brother as he wrestles with his. There are not always easy answers, and we don't know how we would respond in someone else's situation. I also believe we need to come face to face with reality. The developed side of the wall is a land of "telephone poles." We have more options than any previous generation had, and we need spiritual discernment to make Kingdom-focused choices. But we do find other cultures that struggled with affluence, and one of those was the city of Sodom. Sodom, like our modern culture, was filled with all manner of immorality, and its citizens had brazenly turned their backs on God.

But in analyzing Sodom, the prophet Ezekiel observed something that should sober us as we consider the similarities in our cultures. The prophet said, "Behold, this was the iniquity of thy sister Sodom, pride, fullness of bread, and abundance of idleness was in her and in her daughters, neither did she strengthen the hand of the poor and needy."[b] May this assessment never be true of us!

---

[b] Ezekiel 16:49

Where Do We Go From Here?

It was just another cool November night in 2011 as Ryan Swartz cruised down the dark country road making his rounds. Ryan was a deputy for the sheriff's department of Huron County, Michigan, and as his headlights picked up the outline of a deer on the road ahead, he instinctively slowed his cruiser and scanned the horizon for others. This part of Michigan has many deer, and seeing one on the road was certainly not unusual. But as Ryan approached this one standing in the middle of the road, he couldn't help but be intrigued. It didn't move!

Pulling over to the side of the road with his lights on the deer, Ryan continued to watch. He first thought someone had placed a fake deer out on the road as a prank, wanting to see how people would respond. But Ryan could see some small movement, so finally, wanting to clear the roadway, Deputy Ryan got out of his car and began walking toward the deer.

"I figured as I walked up to it," Swartz said later, "it would just run off the road, and it just stood still. It wasn't moving at all. So I went up and I petted it and I was thinking that would get the deer off the road."[1]

But even as Ryan stood there in the middle of the road petting this deer and scratching behind its ears, the deer refused to budge! So now what should he do? His officer's training had never addressed this situation. After about thirty minutes, Ryan picked up the deer and carried it to the side of the road.

Now on the side of the road, with the cruiser video camera recording all this strange activity, Ryan continued to pet the deer. Finally, after another ten minutes, the deer suddenly came to itself, remembered what deer are supposed to do, and sprinted off into the woods. In one sense this deer was the classic example of being "frozen like a deer caught in the headlights." Yet more was going on than just a typical deer responding to a bright light. Wildlife experts who watched the video and heard the deputy's report have said the only reason a deer would stand immobile like that was because of a previous trauma. Very likely this deer had recently experienced a close call or sudden shock involving vehicle headlights, and fear had caused it to freeze.

Freezing From Fear

As I look back at the times I have tried to help people, only to discover later that my efforts were ineffective or even detrimental, I have found myself freezing like a deer in the headlights. I can think of times when I gave money to someone asking for help, only to later discover the person had lied and used the funds for something I never would have endorsed. And when remembering past failures, it is possible to stop sharing out of fear of doing it wrong again. But it is important to not stop giving and helping due to fear of failure.

So how can we overcome this fear and encourage healthy giving in our lives? How can we actually bless those in need rather than unknowingly harm them? And most important, how can we be good stewards of what God has placed in our care and share His resources as He would wish? In this final chapter we want to look at some answers to these questions and some basic steps we can take to keep moving toward godly giving.

- **The need to give:** While God intends that we share with a primary desire to bless those in need, it is also imperative to begin with an understanding of our need to give. We desperately need to share for our own spiritual wellbeing, so don't let fear of failure keep you from giving. We can become sick from an unbalanced diet, yet we should not stop eating entirely. Giving, whether of time or other resources, is just as essential to our spiritual lives as eating is to our physical bodies. Just as a pond with no outlet will grow stagnant

> *We desperately need to share for our own spiritual wellbeing.*

and begin to stink, so our spiritual lives will deteriorate rapidly if we do not continue to pass blessing on to others.

- **Give wisely:** Jesus told the religious leaders of His day that even though they went to great lengths to reach out to people, it would have been better if they had just stayed home. He said, "Ye compass sea and land to make one proselyte [religious convert], and when he is made, ye make him twofold more the child of hell than yourselves."[a] These men worked hard and probably believed they were doing much good. But Jesus said in reality they were doing more harm than good. Paul told the church at Corinth that it is important to give in a way that "no man should blame us in this abundance which is administered by us."[b]

  There is a tendency in our materialistic culture to react and assume that the definition of Biblical stewardship is disposing of stuff. If hanging on to too many things is evil, we reason, then the more we can get rid of, the holier we will be. But remember, good stewardship isn't about dumping possessions. It is about using God's resources as He wants us to. This will mean giving thought to how we share, and taking time to discern the will of the Lord. God has not given us only stuff, He has also given us the ability to reason and make intelligent choices.

- **Give prayerfully:** As we begin to follow the Scriptural injunction to consider the poor and use wisdom in our giving, we soon realize our need of help—divine help! Providing real and lasting assistance to those who are struggling isn't easy, and it is essential to understand our great need for divine guidance. Pray for discernment as you try to decide who and how to assist. Earlier we went through some steps to discernment, but remember, you will never reduce proper discernment to a checklist or flowchart. We don't have all the information,

---

[a] Matthew 23:15

[b] 2 Corinthians 8:20

and we can't see others' hearts. We have trouble discerning impure motives in our own heart, so how can we be sure we have good insight into the heart of another? And don't stop praying after you give. Pray for the individuals who receive help, and if you give through an organization, pray for the staff administering the aid. They daily face difficult decisions.

- **Appreciate diversity within the body of Christ:** Paul, in writing to the church at Corinth, reminded them of the differing gifts God has placed within the church. "Now there are diversities of gifts, but the same Spirit. And there are differences of administrations, but the same Lord. And there are diversities of operations, but it is the same God that worketh all in all."[c] God not only created diversity, but He uses it within the church in reaching out to others. God does not call us all to the same task, and we don't all have the same abilities or burdens. Learn to appreciate the gifts and burdens of others. It is tempting to assume that others within my fellowship should share the burden God has given me. But much energy is lost in the body of Christ when we view our projects, burdens, and even organizations as competing with others. Some may feel a strong burden to help local shut-ins, and others may be called to foreign lands. Even though you may not share the same burden as your brother, if he is actively building the Kingdom of God, learn to appreciate his work and encourage him in it. Understand as well that there is no silver bullet when dealing with long-term poverty. The root cause of all poverty is sin, and the answer is Jesus Christ. But there are a variety of ways to provide sustainable blessing. Even though you may feel called to help in a certain way, be willing to bless and learn from others.

- **Fear cynicism:** One of my greatest concerns in helping the needy is cynicism within my heart. That pessimistic, skeptical attitude that tends to creep in after being burnt several times

---

[c] 1 Corinthians 12:4-6

in a row is destructive. Yesterday I stopped to fill my vehicle with fuel, and there, standing at the nearest intersection, was a man holding a gas can. On the can was a homemade sign proclaiming his need for fuel. I immediately doubted the actual need. It seemed he had placed himself just far enough from the gas station to make it difficult for anyone pumping gas to assess his need, and I began to suspect he just wanted money to use for something else. But the fact is, I was in a hurry and didn't want to take the time to go talk to him, and I felt cynical about his motives and integrity. These thoughts went through my mind as I pumped gas, but I finally became disgusted enough with my own lack of concern that I went and talked to him and ended up filling his gas can. Did I do the right thing? I may never know, but I do need to constantly battle cynicism. It creeps in gradu-

> *We need to fear cynicism more than the loss of time or money.*

ally, and I can become adept at explaining it away. We need to fear it more than the loss of time or money.

- **Be willing to admit past mistakes:** One of the hardest things for us to do is admit our failures. When working with the poor, we will do the wrong thing at times. It isn't a question of if, but when. But the real question is, how will you respond to those failures? This question is pertinent not only to individuals but to charitable organizations as well. In the last few years there has been a growing awareness of the need to learn from failure. In April of 2010, an event called FailFaire was held in New York City.[2] FailFaire was a gathering of humanitarian aid organizations that were invited to come and share their worst failures. In describing the purpose of these meetings, founder Katrin Verclas said, "Development is a field with finite resources, and so the less money we waste the better. And part of that is learning from the things that didn't work, so that we don't endlessly repeat them."[3] Some organizations, like *Engineers Without Borders of Canada,* even publish a regular Failure Report[4] in an attempt to help others avoid the mistakes they have made. These are just secular humanitarian organizations who understand the need to learn from past mistakes. How much more should we as followers of Jesus be willing to confess that we fail at times in our attempts to help others. This can be embarrassing, but we want to work in a way that God will bless.

- **Use the resources God provides:** Whether sharing literature to move people to a life-changing relationship with Jesus Christ, using the local church to spread the Gospel, or sharing the resources God has placed in your care, give it your best, realizing that God has put you in this period of time for a specific purpose. Having a Kingdom-focused vision of life will enable you to see these resources from God's perspective and will encourage proper stewardship. There is so much need; we cannot afford to let these resources lie idle.

- **Don't give up!** It is so easy to subconsciously give up, to conclude that the risk of failure is too high, and that many don't really want help anyway. But I want to point you to an observation the Apostle John made. He said that as Jesus gathered His disciples around Him in the upper room, "He loved them unto the end."[d] Whom did Jesus love unto the end? These men had caused Jesus a lot of trouble since He had first started working with them. They had continually tried to jockey for leadership in the coming Kingdom, had just finished yet another argument about who was the greatest, and within a few hours would all forsake Him and run. But even more than this, the very next verse begins to tell about the activities of Judas Iscariot. He was within minutes of betraying Jesus, yet Jesus chose to love him as well as the other disciples! I often think about Jesus and Judas's relationship. I think Jesus taught,

---

[d] John 13:1

loved, and treated Judas just like He did the other disciples, yet Jesus also knew where Judas was heading.

I like to help people if I am fairly sure they will respond as I think they should. I enjoy reaching out if the results seem guaranteed. But I so easily dismiss a person if I see little hope of my efforts bearing fruit. However, the message of Jesus is clear—go ahead and give. Give of your abilities, give of your resources, and give freely of your time. Don't expect anything in return for your efforts, and don't give up!

Conclusion

So often, overcome by past mistakes and fear of future failure, I become ineffective. Like the deer standing in the middle of the road, I become fearful that if I reach out to that homeless person, I may be "taken" again. But God has placed great blessing in our path. If you live on the stuffed side of the wall, you have opportunity to bless in a way believers in the past—and many today—could only dream of. So use the opportunities God has placed before you. Reach out to the struggling ones in your own congregation, your community, and beyond. Perhaps Paul's words to the church at Corinth have never been so applicable. Paul encouraged them to share with poor believers living in another country: "That now at this time your abundance may be a supply for their want, that their abundance may also be a supply for your want; that there may be equality."[e] May the Lord bless you as you reach over the wall and wisely share what God has placed in your care.

---

[e] 2 Corinthians 8:14

Endnotes

Chapter One

[1] Carol Morello, "Census: Middle Class Shrinks to an All-Time Low," *The Washington Post,* September 12, 2012, <http://www.washingtonpost.com/business/economy/poverty-was-flat-in-2011-percentage-without-health-insurance-fell/2012/09/12/0e04632c-fc29-11e1-8adc-499661afe377_story.html>, accessed on November 15, 2012.

[2] <http://finance.yahoo.com/tech-ticker/the-u.s.-middle-class-is-being-wiped-out-here's-the-stats-to-prove-it-520657.html>, accessed on October 6, 2011.

[3] "Nearly Half of Americans Report Giving Less to Charity in 2010," December 22, 2010, <http://www.angus-reid.com/polls/43688/nearly-half-of-americans-report-giving-less-to-charity-in-2010>, accessed on October 6, 2011.

Chapter Two

[1] Judy Keen, "Unraveling the Mystery of Why We Give, or Don't," USA Today, November 29, 2010.

[2] Karl Barth, Church Dogmatics, T & T Clark International, New York, 1956, p. 41.

Chapter Three

[1] Kevin Gray, "The King of Hollywood Philanthropy," Details, November 30, 2010, <http://www.details.com/culture-trends/critical-eye/201012/humanitarian-power-broker-trevor-neilson-global-philanthropy-group#ixzz1Y7wRCGnz>, accessed on September 16, 2011.

[2] Nora Boustany, "Hollywood Stars Find an Audience for Social Causes," The Washington Post, June 10, 2007, <http://www.washingtonpost.com/wp-dyn/content/article/2007/06/09/AR2007060901516.html>, accessed on September 16, 2011.

Chapter Four

[1] Lois Beckett, "By the Numbers: Life and Death at Foxconn," *ProPublica,* January 27, 2012, <http://www.propublica.org/article/by-the-numbers-life-and-death-at-foxconn>, accessed on November 30, 2012.

[2] Sophia Cheng, "The Deadly Labor Behind Our Phones, Laptops, and Consumer Gadgets," September 1, 2011, <http://colorlines.com/archives/2011/09/the_deadly_labor_of_consumer_electronics.html>, accessed on September 20, 2011.

[3] "Dying Young: Suicide and China's Booming Economy," May 25, 2010, <http://sacom.hk/wp-content/uploads/2010/05/dying-young_sucide-chinas-booming-economy.pdf>, accessed on September 20, 2011.

[4] Chi-Chi Zhang, "Apple Manufacturing Plant Workers Complain of Long Hours, Militant Culture," *CNN,* February 6, 2012, <http://www.cnn.com/2012/02/06/world/asia/china-apple-foxconn-worker/index.html>, accessed on November 15, 2012.

[5] Gene Edward Veith, "Who Gives Two Cents for Missions?" *World,* October 22, 2005, <http://www.worldmag.com/articles/11176>, accessed on September 22, 2011.

Chapter Five

[1] Jeff Gelman, <http://www.nationalhomeless.org/faces/article1.html>, accessed on October 1, 2011.

Chapter Six

[1] Oliver Lee, "Does Your Surgeon Have a Drinking Problem?" February 23, 2012, <http://www.takepart.com/article/2012/02/23/does-your-doctor-have-drinking-problem>, accessed on March 13, 2012.

[2] Jeffrey Gettleman, "Contractors Are Accused in Large-Scale Theft of Food Aid in Somalia," *The New York Times,* August 16, 2011, <http://www.nytimes.com/2011/08/17/world/africa/17somalia.html>, accessed on January 10, 2012.

[3] "A Stuck Elevator," *Courier-Journal,* January 9, 2012, <http://www.courier-journal.com/article/20120110/OPINION01/301100014/Census-data-mobility-gap-United-States-New-York-Times-income?odyssey=mod%7Cnewswell%7Ctext%7CHome%7Cs>, accessed on January 10, 2012.

Chapter Seven

[1] Bryant L. Myers, *Walking With The Poor,* Orbis Books, Maryknoll, N.Y., 2007, p. 27.

[2] New Agriculturalist, September 2007, <http://www.new-ag.info/en/country/profile.php?a=202>, accessed on June 26, 2012.

[3] John DeGraaf, David Wann, Thomas Naylor, *Affluenza,* Berrett-Koehler Publishers, San Francisco, 2001, p. 2.

[4] Gerald Celente, quoted by John DeGraaf, David Wann, Thomas Naylor in *Affluenza,* Berrett-Koehler Publishers, 2002, < http://www.philosophicalsociety.com/Archives/affluenza.htm#I. Interesting Justapositions by Gerald Celente>, accessed on February 9, 2012.

[5] Joan Ryan, "Why Gore Is Right to Carry On," *San Francisco Chronicle,* December 5, 2000.

Chapter Eight

[1] Steve Corbett & Brian Fikkert, *When Helping Hurts,* Moody Publishers, Chicago, 2009, p. 33.

[2] *The Ante-Nicene Fathers,* Vol. 4, Eerdmans Publishing Company, Grand Rapids, 1989, p. 179.

³ David Bercot, *The Kingdom That Turned the World Upside Down*, Scroll Publishing, Amberson, Pa., p. 35.

Chapter Nine

¹ Ralph Waldo Emerson, "Self-Reliance," *Essays and Lectures*, Library of America, New York, 1983, pp. 261-262.
² Randy Alcorn, *Money, Possessions, and Eternity*, Tyndale House, Wheaton, Ill., 1989, p.248.
³ Brian Rice, "Mother Teresa—A Few Gems to Ponder," January 24, 2009, <http://lci.typepad.com/leaders_resourcing_leader/2009/01/mother-teresa---a-few-gems-to-ponder.html>, accessed on February 21, 2012.
⁴ *The Ante-Nicene Fathers*, Vol. 2, Eerdmans Publishing Company, Grand Rapids, 1989, p. 268.

Chapter Ten

¹ Canal de Panamá, <http://www.pancanal.com/eng/general/canal-faqs/index.html>, accessed on February 13, 2012.
² Robert C. Kennedy, "The First Mountain to Be Removed," *The New York Times* and *HarpWeek*, July 22, 2001, <http://tv.nytimes.com/learning/general/onthisday/harp/0722.html>, accessed on February 13, 2012.
³ Centers for Disease Control and Prevention, "The History of Malaria, an Ancient Disease," <http://www.cdc.gov/malaria/about/history/>, accessed on June 26, 2012.

Chapter Eleven

¹ Dambisa Moyo, "Why Foreign Aid Is Hurting Africa," *The Wall Street Journal*, March 21, 2009, <http://online.wsj.com/article/SB123758895999200083.html>, accessed on February 14, 2012.
² Abby Shields, <http://www.abbyshields.com/>, accessed on July 19, 2012.

Chapter Twelve

¹ Tom O'Neill, "Untouchable," *National Geographic Magazine*, June 2003, <http://ngm.nationalgeographic.com/ngm/0306/feature1/>, accessed on February 14, 2012.
² Jonathan Martin, *Giving Wisely?* Last Chapter Publishing, Sisters, Oreg., 2008, pp. 13-14, 122-123.

Chapter Thirteen

¹ Index Mundi, <http://www.indexmundi.com/g/r.aspx?t=0&v=67&l=en>, accessed on February 16, 2012.
² Jason Deparle, "Preaching Free-Market Gospel to Skeptical Africa," *The New York Times*, November 18, 2006, <http://www.nytimes.com/2006/11/18/us/politics/18thinktank.html?pagewanted=1&adxnnlx=1329411893-pxj6JCM4azpRstJo4gGS9Q>, accessed on February 16, 2012.
³ Steve Corbett & Brian Fikkert, *When Helping Hurts*, Moody Publishers, Chicago, 2009, p. 115.

Chapter Fifteen

[1] Emily Smith, " 'Blind Mules' Unknowingly Ferry Drugs Across the U.S-Mexico Border," *CNN*, January 24, 2012, <http://www.cnn.com/2012/01/23/world/americas/mexico-blind-drug-mules/index.html>, accessed on February 28, 2012.
[2] Philip Jenkins, *The Next Christendom: The Coming Globalization of Christianity*, Oxford University Press, New York, 2002, p. 37.
[3] Joann Van Engen, "The Cost of Short-Term Missions," *Catapult Magazine*, Vol. 4, No. 21, November 18, 2005, <https://www.catapultmagazine.com/global-eyes/article/cost-of-short-term-missions>, accessed on February 28, 2012.
[4] Glenn Schwartz, "How Short-Term Missions Can Go Wrong," *International Journal of Frontier Missions*, Spring 2004, <http://www.ijfm.org/PDFs_IJFM/21_1_PDFs/27_34_Schwartz.pdf>, accessed on February 28, 2012.
[5] Brother Yun & Paul Hattaway, *Back to Jerusalem*, Biblica Publishing, Colorado Springs, 2003, p. 101.

Chapter Sixteen

[1] Peter Hoover, *The Mystery of the Mark*, Elmendorf Books, Mountain Lake, Minn., 2008, p. 11.
[2] Carl F. Bowman, *Brethren Society*, The John Hopkins University Press, Baltimore, 1995, p. 96.
[3] Stephen Protheros, "Religious Literacy," *U.S. News & World Report*, April 9, 2007.
[4] <http://www.goodreads.com/quotes/show/160312>, accessed on February 27, 2012.
[5] J.J. (Dons) Kritzinger, "The Rwandan Tragedy as Public Indictment Against Christian Mission," *Missionalia*, October 2009, <http://www.oocities.org/missionalia/rwanda1.htm>, accessed on February 27, 2012.

Chapter Seventeen

[1] Michael, Luo, "For Exercise in New York Futility, Push Button," The New York Times, February 27, 2004, <http://www.nytimes.com/2004/02/27/nyregion/for-exercise-in-new-york-futility-push-button.html>, accessed on February 29, 2012.
[2] Randy Alcorn, Money, Possessions, and Eternity, Tyndale House Publishers, Wheaton, Ill., 1989, p. 259.

Chapter Eighteen

[1] "Emmons Shoots Wrong Target, Loses Gold Medal on Last Shot," August 22, 2004, <http://nbcsports.msnbc.com/id/5785670/ns/sports-other_sports/>, accessed on March 1, 2012.
[2] Peter Worthington, "The Problem with Foreign Aid," *Toronto Sun,* August 6, 2011, <http://www.torontosun.com/2011/08/06/the-problem-with-foreign-aid>, accessed on March 9, 2012.

Chapter Twenty-One

[1] Steve Corbett & Brian Fikkert, *When Helping Hurts*, Moody Publishers, Chicago, 2009, p. 105.

² Christina Rexrode, "Haiti Volunteer Travel Takes More Than Good Intentions," August 4, 2011, <http://www.nbcnews.com/id/44018778/ns/travel-destination_travel/t/haiti-volunteer-travel-takes-more-good-intentions/#.UcSyS_nVDzw>, accessed on March 6, 2012.

Chapter Twenty-Two
¹ Demo Hassan, "For 40 Years, Food Has Been Routine," *Irin,* August 26, 2011, <http://www.irinnews.org/Report/93592/KENYA-Demo-Hassan-For-40-years-food-aid-has-been-routine>, accessed on March 7, 2012.
² Roland Bunch, *Two Ears of Corn,* World Neighbors, Oklahoma City, 1982, p. 19.
³ Bryant L. Myers, *Walking With the Poor,* Orbis Books, Maryknoll, N.Y., 1999, p. 130.
⁴ Demo Hassan, "For 40 Years, Food Has Been Routine," *Irin,* August 26, 2011, <http://www.irinnews.org/Report/93592/KENYA-Demo-Hassan-For-40-years-food-aid-has-been-routine>, accessed on March 7, 2012.

Chapter Twenty-Three
¹ Jan Stravers, "A Handful of Rice," August 24, 2009, <http://www.crcna.org/news.cfm?newsid=1481>, accessed on March 8, 2012.
² Bryant L. Myers, *Walking With the Poor,* Orbis Books, Maryknoll, N.Y., 1999, p. 176.
³ Peter Greer & Phil Smith, *The Poor Will Be Glad,* Zondervan, Grand Rapids, 2009, p. 58.
⁴ Steve Corbett & Brian Fikkert, *When Helping Hurts,* Moody Publishers, Chicago, 2009, p. 127.
⁵ "A Handful of Rice," video from International Steward, <http://vimeo.com/16288195>, accessed on March 8, 2012.

Chapter Twenty-Four
¹ "Grace of Giving in Uganda," video from International Steward, <http://graceof-giving.net/bishop_hannington>, accessed on March 9, 2012.
² Steve Saint, "Projecting Poverty Where It Doesn't Exist," *Mission Frontiers,* Sept./Oct. 2011, <www.missionfrontiers.org>, accessed on March 9, 2012.

Chapter Twenty-Five
¹ Muhammad Yunus, *Banker to the Poor,* Public Affairs, New York, 1999, p. 48.
² William Easterly, *The White Man's Burden,* The Penguin Press, New York, 2006, p. 6.
³ Jonathan Martin, *Giving Wisely?* Last Chapter Publishing, Sisters Oreg., 2008, pp. 158-159.

Chapter Twenty-Six
¹ "Warren Buffet," *Forbes,* March 2013, <http://www.forbes.com/profile/warren-buf-fett/>, accessed on November 30, 2012.

[2] Walter B. Knight, *Knight's Master Book of New Illustrations,* Eerdmans Publishing Company, Ann Arbor, Mich., 1956, p. 248.

Chapter Twenty-Eight

[1] George W. Peters, "The Church in Missions," *Bibliotheca Sacra,* Vol. BSAC 125:497 (Jan 1968), <http://www.galaxie.com/article/bsac125-497-05>, accessed on July 13, 2012.

[2] George Peters, *A Biblical Theology of Missions,* The Moody Bible Institute, Chicago, 1972, pp. 216-217.

Chapter Thirty

[1] Lisa Lindsey, "Deputy Carries Frightened Deer Off Road," November 17, 2011, <http://my947.com/deputy-carries-frightened-deer-off-road-video/http://www.fox17online.com/fox17-video-shots-deer-in-headlights-carried-off-road-20111115,0,1275006.htmlstory>, accessed on July 18, 2012.

[2] Stephanie Strom, "Nonprofits Review Technology Failures," *The New York Times,* August 16, 2010, <http://www.nytimes.com/2010/08/17/technology/17fail.html>, accessed on July 19, 2012.

[3] "Getting NGOs to Celebrate Failure, So They Can Learn From Others' Mistakes," orated by Alex Villarreal, uploaded on October 8, 2010, <http://failfaire.org/http://www.youtube.com/watch?v=C8PXk8Vdp1s>, accessed on July 19, 2012.

[4] Madeleine Bunting, "NGO Hopes to Benefit From Failure," January 17, 2011, <http://www.guardian.co.uk/global-development/poverty-matters/2011/jan/17/ngos-failure-mistakes-learn-encourage>, accessed on July 19, 2012.

About the Author

Gary Miller was raised in an Anabaptist community in California and today lives with his wife Patty and family in the Pacific Northwest. Gary desires to encourage Christians in developed countries to share their resources and focus more on the Kingdom of God. He also continues to work with the poor in developing countries and manages the SALT Microfinance Solutions program for Christian Aid Ministries. This program offers business and spiritual teaching to those living in chronic poverty, provides small loans, and assists them in learning how to use their God-given resources to become sustainable.

Gary's enthusiasm for Kingdom building has prompted him to write the Kingdom-Focused Living series. *The Other Side of the Wall* is his fourth book in the series. He also continues to write teaching manuals for developing countries. See page 243 for a list of his published works.

Have you been inspired by Gary's materials? Maybe you have questions? Perhaps you even disagree with the author? Share your thoughts by sending an e-mail to kingdomfinance@camoh.org or writing to Christian Aid Ministries, P.O. Box 360, Berlin, Ohio 44610.

Additional Resources
by Gary Miller

Kingdom-Focused Finances for the Family
This first book in the Kingdom-Focused Living series is realistic, humorous, and serious about getting us to become stewards instead of owners.

Charting a Course in Your Youth
A serious call to youth to examine their faith, focus, and finances.

Going Till You're Gone
A plea for godly examples—for older men and women who will demonstrate a Kingdom-focused vision all the way to the finish line.

Budgeting Made Simple
A budgeting workbook in a ring binder; complements *Kingdom-Focused Finances for the Family*.

Small Business Handbook
A manual used in microfinance programs in Third World countries. Includes devotionals and practical business teaching. Ideal for missions and churches.

AUDIO BOOKS, NARRATED BY THE AUTHOR

Kingdom-Focused Finances for the Family, Charting a Course in Your Youth, Going Till You're Gone, and *The Other Side of the Wall.*

AUDIO AND POWER POINT SEMINARS

Kingdom-Focused Finances Seminar—3 audio CDs
This three-session seminar takes you beyond our culture's view of money and possessions, and challenges you to examine your heart by looking at your treasure.

Kingdom-Focused Finances Seminar Audio PowerPoint—3 CDs
With the visual aid included on these CDs, you can now follow along on the slides Gary uses in his seminars while you listen to the presentation. A good tool for group study or individual use. A computer is needed to view these CDs.

Bibliography

Author's Note: I would be extremely presumptuous to write a book like this without acknowledging my heavy dependence on others. I am greatly indebted to the many who shared both verbally and in writing what they learned in working with poverty and relief.

Books on Helping the Poor Effectively

Befus, David R., *Where There Are No Jobs: Enterprise Solutions for Employment for the Poor,* Published by LAM, Miami, 2005.
> The author worked on many relief and development projects in various countries. The book encourages the use of enterprise to create employment and self-sustaining communities.

Bunch, Roland, *Two Ears of Corn: A Guide to People-Centered Agricultural Improvement,* World Neighbors, Oklahoma City, 1982.
> This easy-to-read book focuses on sustainability in agriculture.

Collins, Daryl, Jonathan Morduch, Stuart Rutherford, Orlanda Ruthven, *Port folios of the Poor: How the World's Poor Live on $2 a Day,* Princeton University Press, Princeton, N.J., 2009.
> The authors spent a year tracking extremely poor families around the globe to see how they manage their personal finances. A good book but written in a scholarly manner that is harder to read. If you are willing to wade through the material, it shows how much ingenuity it takes to live on $2 a day.

Corbett, Steve, and Brian Fikkert, *When Helping Hurts: How to Alleviate Poverty Without Hurting the Poor . . . and Yourself,* Moody Publishers, Chicago, 2009.
> Excellent book on how to alleviate poverty without hurting the poor and yourself in the process. Provides principles that apply locally as well as in foreign countries. If you want to make sure that your help is not actually doing damage, this book is valuable.

Corson, Sarah, *Glimpses of God in the Lives of the Poor,* SIFAT, Lineville, Ala., 2004.
> Encourages us to learn lessons from the poor about God. The author has lived in South America for many years, and the book is filled with inspiring stories.

Easterly, William, *The White Man's Burden: Why the West's Efforts to Aid the Rest Have Done So Much Ill and So Little Good,* The Penguin Press, New York, 2006.
> Exposes some of the failure in large government-driven humanitarian aid, the effects of colonialism, and the historical impact of too much aid given too fast. Encourages smaller projects where we walk beside the poor and help them find local solutions.

Elmer, Duane, *Cross-Cultural Conflict: Building Relationships for Effective Ministry,* InterVarsity Press, Downers Grove, Ill., 1993.
> Addresses the challenges and provides solutions to working within different cultures. A well-written book to help us understand why others react like they do in other countries. Teaches how to reach over cultural differences to build relationships.

Finley, Bob, *Reformation in Foreign Missions,* Christian Aid Mission, Charlottesville, Va., 2005.
> The author looks at many of the problems in cross-cultural mission attempts in the past and makes the case for indigenous missionaries.

Greer, Peter, and Phil Smith, *The Poor Will Be Glad: Joining the Revolution to Lift the World Out of Poverty,* Zondervan Publishing, Grand Rapids, 2009.
> Promotes the microloan and savings group models. Gives many stories of how these programs have helped individuals and communities around the world.

Lai, Patrick, *Tent Making: Business as Missions,* Authentic Media, Waynesboro, Ga., 2005.
> The author has lived in the 10/40 window for many years. Describes the challenges and blessings of using businesses in foreign—and even hostile—countries as a way to reach out.

Lanier, Sarah A., *Foreign to Familiar: A Guide to Understanding Hot and Cold Climate Cultures,* McDougal Publishing, Hagerstown, Md., 2000.
> An interesting book designed to help you see life from the eyes of someone raised in a different culture. Exposes the blind spots all of us have regardless where we have been raised.

Livermore, David A., *Serving With Eyes Wide Open: Doing Short-Term Missions with Cultural Intelligence,* Baker Books, Grand Rapids, 2006.
> A helpful book if you are interested in short-term missions. The author draws on personal experience to expose potential problems with these

efforts and goes on to share some solutions. A good book to give to young people before they travel.

Martin, Jonathan, *Giving Wisely?: Killing With Kindness or Empowering Lasting Transformation?,* Last Chapter Publishing, Sisters, Oreg., 2008.
An easy-to-read book on creating lasting transformation in communities. It teaches methods to promote lasting change and shows how that much of our giving creates problems.

Moyo, Dambisa, *Dead Aid: Why Aid Is Not Working and How There Is a Better Way for Africa,* Farrar, Straus, and Giroux, New York, 2009.
The author was raised in Zambia and observed firsthand some of the problems with indiscriminate aid. Promotes using enterprise to create long-term change in countries with chronic poverty.

Myers, Bryant L., *Walking With the Poor: Principles and Practices of Transformational Development,* Orbis Books, Maryknoll, New York, 2007.
An excellent book on development. It is written in a scholarly manner and is used as a textbook in courses promoting Christian development with a focus on sustainability.

Schwartz, Glenn J., *When Charity Destroys Dignity: Overcoming Unhealthy Dependency in the Christian Movement,* World Mission Associates, Lancaster, Pa., 2007.
The author has many years of experience in helping churches in developing countries become self-supporting. The book encourages us to help people find and develop the resources God has placed in their care.

Sider, Ronald J., *Rich Christians in an Age of Hunger: Moving from Affluence to Generosity,* Word Publishing, Dallas, 1997.
Written from a Protestant perspective, this book has a great deal of information on the causes of poverty. It encourages the reader to acknowledge that God intends for us to use "our" resources to bless others.

Smith, Phil and Eric Thurman, *A Billion Bootstraps: Microcredit, Barefoot Banking, and the Business Solution for Ending Poverty,* McGraw Hill Companies, New York, 2007.
This is a book written to promote microcredit. It has a lot of information regarding the advantages of microloans. While it may oversell the concept as the ultimate tool for poverty alleviation, it does provide good information for the uninformed. Appeals to the businessman.

Other Resources Promoting Sustainability

Chalmers Institute – Lookout Mountain, GA
http://www.chalmers.org
Chalmers Institute provides many resources, books, teaching aids, seminars, and opportunity for people working in developing countries to network. They have online courses to help those living in these countries teach sustainable solutions. Chalmers approaches microfinance from a Christian perspective.

CGAP
http://www.cgap.org
CGAP is an online resource where you can find recent studies, forms which can be used in microfinance, and many statistics. It is a secular site dedicated to poverty alleviation, industry trends, and promoting financial access for the world's poor. Can be a good resource in developing new sustainable programs.

Microfinance Gateway
http://www.microfinancegateway.org
Another site maintained by CGAP that provides more information regarding the latest studies, publications, and resources available. The information is not from a Christian perspective, but can be a good source for research.

The Way to God and Peace

We live in a world contaminated by sin. Sin is anything that goes against God's holy standards. When we do not follow the guidelines that God our Creator gave us, we are guilty of sin. Sin separates us from God, the source of life.

Since the time when the first man and woman, Adam and Eve, sinned in the Garden of Eden, sin has been universal. The Bible says that we all have "sinned and come short of the glory of God" (Romans 3:23). It also says that the natural consequence for that sin is eternal death, or punishment in an eternal hell: "Then when lust hath conceived, it bringeth forth sin: and sin, when it is finished, bringeth forth death" (James 1:15).

But we do not have to suffer eternal death in hell. God provided forgiveness for our sins through the death of His only Son, Jesus Christ. Because Jesus was perfect and without sin, He could die in our place. "For God so loved the world that he gave his only begotten Son, that whosoever believeth in him should not perish, but have everlasting life" (John 3:16).

A sacrifice is something given to benefit someone else. It costs the giver greatly. Jesus was God's sacrifice. Jesus' death takes away the penalty of sin for everyone who accepts this sacrifice and truly repents of their sins. To repent of sins means to be truly sorry for and turn away from the things we have done that have violated God's standards. (Acts 2:38; 3:19).

Jesus died, but He did not remain dead. After three days, God's Spirit miraculously raised Him to life again. God's Spirit does something similar in us. When we receive Jesus as our sacrifice and repent of our sins, our hearts are changed. We become spiritually alive! We develop new desires and attitudes (2 Corinthians 5:17). We begin to make choices that please God (1 John 3:9). If we do fail and commit sins, we can ask God for forgiveness. "If we confess our sins, he is faithful and just to forgive us our sins, and to cleanse us from all unrighteousness" (1 John 1:9).

Once our hearts have been changed, we want to continue growing spiritually. We will be happy to let Jesus be the Master of our lives and will want to become more like Him. To do this, we must meditate on God's Word and commune with God in prayer. We will testify to others of this change by being baptized and sharing the good news of God's victory over sin and death. Fellowship with a faithful group of believers will strengthen our walk with God (1 John 1:7).